STUDY GUIDE

UNL🔒CKING THE CODE OF THE SUPERNATURAL

THE SECRET TO GOD'S POWER IN YOU

KYNAN BRIDGES

WHITAKER
HOUSE

Unless otherwise indicated, all Scripture quotations are taken from the *King James Version Easy Read Bible*, KJVER®, © 2001, 2007, 2010, 2015 by Whitaker House. Used by permission. All rights reserved. Scripture quotations marked (NKJV) are taken from the *New King James Version*, © 1979, 1980, 1982 by Thomas Nelson, Inc. Used by permission. All rights reserved.

Some definitions of Greek words are taken from the New Testament Greek Lexicon—King James Version or New American Standard, based on Thayer's and Smith's Bible Dictionary, plus others (public domain), www.BibleStudyTools.com. Some definitions of Hebrew words are taken from the Old Testament Hebrew Lexicon—King James Version or New American Standard, which is the Brown, Driver, Briggs, Gesenius Lexicon (public domain), BibleStudyTools.com. Other Greek and Hebrew definitions are taken from the electronic version of *Strong's Exhaustive Concordance of the Bible*, STRONG, (© 1980, 1986, and assigned to World Bible Publishers, Inc. Used by permission. All rights reserved.).

Unless otherwise indicated, all dictionary definitions are taken from Lexico.com, Oxford University Press, © 2020.

UNLOCKING THE CODE OF THE SUPERNATURAL STUDY GUIDE

The Secret to God's Power in You

Kynan Bridges Ministries, Inc.
P.O. Box 159
Ruskin, FL 33575
www.kynanbridges.com
info@kynanbridges.com

ISBN: 978-1-64123-626-3
eBook ISBN: 978-1-64123-627-0
Printed in the United States of America
© 2021 by Kynan Bridges

Whitaker House
1030 Hunt Valley Circle
New Kensington, PA 15068
www.whitakerhouse.com

1 2 3 4 5 6 7 8 9 10 11 ⨆ 28 27 26 25 24 23 22 21

CONTENTS

HOW TO USE THIS STUDY GUIDE

Welcome to *Unlocking the Code of the Supernatural Study Guide: The Secret to God's Power in You*. We are delighted that you have made the decision to dig deeper into God's Word. This study guide is designed as a stand-alone biblical study on the theme of believers' identity and power in Christ. The course may be completed independently by individual students or may be used in a group setting, such as a Bible study, a Sunday school class, a course on the foundations of the Christian faith, or a prayer group.

ELEMENTS OF EACH LESSON

Chapter Theme

The main idea of each chapter is summarized for emphasis and clarity.

Questions for Reflection

Thought questions are posed as a warm-up to lead into the study. (For group study, these questions may be asked before or after reading the "Chapter Theme," at the discretion of the leader.)

Exploring Principles and Purposes

Questions and review material are provided to summarize and highlight the principles and truths within each chapter and begin to lead the reader/group participant to personalize what is being studied. Page numbers from the *Unlocking the Code of the Supernatural* book corresponding to the answers to each question are supplied for easy reference. (An answer key for the "Exploring Principles and Purposes" questions may be found beginning on page 105.)

Conclusion

A summary or implication statement is included to put the theme of the chapter into perspective.

Applying Principles of the Supernatural

Thought-provoking questions and suggestions for personal action and prayer are provided to help the individual/group participant apply the study material to their particular life circumstances. This section includes three parts:

- Thinking It Over
- Acting on It
- Praying About It

Miracle Testimony

Testimonies are included to give glory to God and encourage the reader to walk in the supernatural.

INTRODUCTION

Through my ministry to thousands of Christians, I have found that many believers don't have a clear understanding of what it means to be new creations in Christ. When we lack this understanding, we block the flow of God's Spirit within us. God wants us to live a supernatural lifestyle, full of His grace and power. Being born again means that the DNA of our heavenly Father is written in our spirit-man. When we fully comprehend this truth, we will be dangerously new creations!

That's why I wrote *Unlocking the Code of the Supernatural*. I want to see believers' lives transformed as they begin to understand that there is no greater way to live a life of victory than to walk according to the Spirit of God. I want to see the church transformed as believers are filled with God's love and power. I want to see the fallen world around us drawn to Christ through the witness of believers who demonstrate that God's power is truly omnipotent.

Unlocking the Code of the Supernatural unveils the various facets of what it means to be a new creation in Christ, highlighting a number of key Scriptures, especially from the Gospels and the Epistles, that relate to this theme. This study guide was developed to help you plant the book's principles deep into your heart and apply them to your circumstances to live a supernatural lifestyle. I have designed these materials so that every believer can be inspired to cast off mistaken ideas about what it means to be a Christian and step into the victory they already have as a brand-new creation in Christ.

I pray that through this study, you will be encouraged to live a life that transcends what you can see and feel so you can tap into a supernatural reality that is so tremendous, it will knock you out of your seat!

PART I:
BIRTHED INTO THE SUPERNATURAL!

FIRST THINGS FIRST

CHAPTER THEME

Frequently, when people accept Christ as their Lord and Savior, they fail to comprehend the full ramifications of their decision. Being a believer is not a religious experience—it is a mystery involving a radical transformation of our spiritual DNA. When we are born again, God gives us a brand-new, supernatural nature that has the power to impact every area of our lives. Only with the Holy Spirit's help can we fully comprehend what it means to have a new life in Christ—and to act on this understanding.

QUESTIONS FOR REFLECTION

1. When you accepted Jesus as your Lord and Savior, what was your conception of what it meant to be a Christian? How has this idea expanded as you've grown in the Lord?

2. What is your current experience of the Christian life? Are you walking in confidence and power, with the knowledge of you who are in Christ?

3. When is the last time you thought of Jesus as the One who holds the very fiber of your being together?

EXPLORING PRINCIPLES AND PURPOSES

1. In the new birth, God has given us an entirely _____-_____,
   _____ nature. (p. 16)

2. What is one dictionary definition of *mystery?* (p.16)

   _____

3. In 1 Corinthians 2:7, what does *"mystery"* from the Greek term *mysterion* mean? (pp. 16–17)

   _____

   _____

4. To whom can the mystery of Christ's new nature be revealed? (p. 17)

   _____

5. Who allows people to comprehend what it means to be born again? (p. 17)

   _____

6. What is one reason so many believers are missing out on a dynamic lifestyle filled with blessing and victory? (p. 17)

   _____

7. There is a correlation between understanding the mystery of the _____ _____
   and _____ _____. (p. 18)

8. What is the secret to unlocking God's power within us? (p. 18)

   _____

9. Based on the discussion of Colossians 1:25–27, what happens when we become new creations? (p. 19)

_____

10. _____ and _____ have done much to shape people's false conceptions of Jesus. (p. 19)

11. Using John 1:1–5 as your source, summarize who Jesus is. (p. 19)

_____

_____

_____

12. Jesus "was _____ _____ _____" and "was _____." Therefore, we know that Jesus was _____ and _____ with the Father. (p. 20)

13. What is the definition of the Greek term *logos*? (p. 20)

_____

14. God created the invisible and visible universe through the person of the living Word, _____ _____. (p. 20)

15. Jesus gives _____, _____, and _____ to everything in creation. (p. 20)

16. What must we do in order to have a genuine relationship with Jesus Christ? (p. 20)

_____

17. From the use of the Greek term *ginomai* in John 1:1–5, we get the sense that Christ is the "_____ _____" by which all things are _____ and _____. (pp. 20–21)

18. In Colossians 1:17, what is the meaning of the word *"consist,"* which comes from the Greek word *synistemi?* (p. 21)

_____

19. Christ is the _____ from which everything has its genesis, and He is also the

_____ _____ by which every fiber of the universe is held together. (p. 21)

20. To what does the Greek term *zoe* (*"life"*) refer in John 1:4? (p. 22)

_____

21. Christ is _____, _____, _____,

_____, _____, and _____ for

humanity. (p. 22)

22. What do we need to understand before we can become "dangerously new creations"? (p. 23)

_____

_____

_____

CONCLUSION

The biblical truths about who Christ is and what it means that He dwells within us by His Holy Spirit have profound implications for living a supernatural lifestyle. Only when we fully understand who Jesus is and what He has done for us can we begin to recognize the supernatural power within ourselves. Christ alone grants us access to the fullness of divine life.

THINKING IT OVER

1. Consider these "Unlocking the Code of the Supernatural Insights" questions from pages 24 and 25 of *Unlocking the Code of the Supernatural*:

   + What is the reason many believers haven't made much progress in understanding the nature of their new birth since their salvation? In what ways might you need to grow in your comprehension of what transpired when you received Jesus?

   + How does the biblical definition of "mystery" compare to the common definition of this term?

   + List some titles that describe the nature of Jesus Christ, based on the first chapter of John.

   + Name some characteristics of the church when it is functioning in the way it is meant to.

2. Does your idea of Jesus align with the description of Him we get from Scripture? How do Jesus's titles help you to understand who He really is?

ACTING ON IT

1. Have you taken the first step in your journey to live supernaturally by receiving Christ as your Lord and Savior? If not, pray the prayer found on page 23 of *Unlocking the Code of the Supernatural*.

2. Spend time reading the gospel of John this week to get to know Jesus better.

PRAYING ABOUT IT

Father, in the name of Jesus Christ, I thank You for who You are and all You have done for me. I believe that Jesus is the Son of God and that, through His blood, I am a new creation. Thank You that my entire purpose for living comes from You. I know that, through Jesus, You created everything that exists, including me. Jesus is my Creator, Definer, Purpose, Sustainer, Life, and Light. Thank You, Lord, for unfolding the mystery of Your wisdom as I release my faith in You and follow Your plans for me. I declare that the mystery of Jesus is unveiled in my spirit. In Jesus's name, amen!

RECEIVING A BRAND-NEW MIND

While I was growing up, I struggled tremendously in school. I was told by the board of education that I had attention deficit hyperactivity disorder (ADHD). I had a very difficult time paying attention and remembering what was taught in class. This led to many problems: I daydreamed all the time. I fought with other students. I was profane.

However, when I gave my life to Christ, something supernatural happened within me. I literally received a new mind. God's DNA was deposited into my very being. After this, I began to think and reason differently. My paradigm changed, and thus my worldview was transformed. I continually reminded myself that I had the mind of Christ. Although some people had told me that I would never graduate from high school, I was supernaturally able to graduate, and I was also accepted at a university. Today, I have several academic degrees, and I have written a number of books. Glory to God for the power of the new creation!

 WHEN WE UNDERSTAND THE TRUTH THAT JESUS CHRIST SHED HIS PRECIOUS BLOOD FOR OUR SINS AND WAS RAISED FROM THE DEAD SO THAT WE COULD WALK IN SUPERNATURAL NEWNESS OF LIFE IN THE POWER OF THE HOLY SPIRIT, WE WILL BE DANGEROUSLY NEW CREATIONS!

A NEW CREATION

CHAPTER THEME

When Scripture speaks of believers as a "new creation," it means that we are brand-new entities, the first of our kind. We are new creations, fresh and vibrant. The very essence and life of God the Father dwells in us. Regeneration has taken place within us, and consequently there is something profoundly new about our inner being. This is the vantage point from which we must reexamine our lives. Yet in order to understand our identity as a new creation, we must have an intimate knowledge of our Creator, which we can only gain through His Word.

QUESTIONS FOR REFLECTION

1. How might the understanding that you are a brand-new creation affect the way you think about yourself and live your life?

2. Many people who have confessed Christ and sincerely desire to have an intimate relationship with Him still deal with habitual sin, addictions, guilt, shame, and condemnation from the past. In what areas are you currently struggling?

3. What does it mean to you that you were created in the image of the triune God?

4. What is ultimately guiding your life decisions—your renewed spirit or your soul?

EXPLORING PRINCIPLES AND PURPOSES

1. What does the Bible refer to when it uses the word *new?* (p. 26)

   _____

2. According to 2 Corinthians 5:17, what is the prerequisite for newness? (p. 28)

   _____

3. Once we are "_____ _____," we can have the assurance that we are a "_____
   _____." (p. 28)

4. What is the meaning of the Greek word *kainos* ("new") in 2 Corinthians 5:17? (p. 28)

   _____

5. What part of our being becomes born again? (p. 28)

   _____

6. From a New Testament perspective, how is the "spirit" defined? (p. 28)

   _____

7. God is a triune Being—_____, _____, and _____
   _____. (p. 29)

8. What happens to our spirit-man when we are born again? (p. 29)

   _____

9. What spiritual access code do we have when we are born again? (p. 29)

   _____

10. What is the meaning of the Greek word *psyche* ("soul")? (p. 30)

_____

11. From what part of our being do we make decisions? (p. 30)

_____

12. The body carries out the _____ and _____ of the soul. (p. 30)

13. When we are born again and our spirit is filled with the life of God, what are we enabled to do? (p. 31)

_____

_____

14. What is one step we can take toward appropriating our new nature through the power of the Holy Spirit? (p. 31)

_____

15. To really know God, we must not only read but also _____ and _____
_____ His Word. (p. 31)

16. What is the essential quality of the spiritual life? (p. 33)

_____

17. Christ is coming back for a bride that is holy, "_____ _____ and
_____." (p. 33)

CONCLUSION

When we are born again, our innermost being is transformed into the image of Jesus Christ Himself. We mirror His very nature. In fact, the very essence and life of God the Father dwells in us. But in order to mirror our heavenly Father, we must spend time getting to know Him through His Word. Only then will we know which attributes of our heavenly Father we should be manifesting as His children.

THINKING IT OVER

1. Consider these "Unlocking the Code of the Supernatural Insights" questions from page 34 of *Unlocking the Code of the Supernatural*:

   * What are the two main qualities of "newness"?

   * What is the prerequisite for spiritual newness?

   * Which part of our being becomes new in the new birth? Which parts need to be brought into alignment with God's nature?

   * What is the access code to our new life in the Spirit?

2. Reflect on a time when you wondered if there was more to the Christian life than what you were experiencing. How has your relationship with God changed since then? In what aspects does it still need to improve?

ACTING ON IT

1. Do you ever blame your bad circumstances on God? Carve out time each morning to pray that God would give you a better understanding of what it means to be a new creation in Christ.

2. Consider starting a gratitude journal that you update daily to remind yourself that the Holy Spirit is living and working in you each day.

PRAYING ABOUT IT

Father, I praise Your holy name for all that You are and all that You have done for me. Thank You that Your Spirit dwells within me. Thank You for empowering me to demonstrate the life of Christ to everyone around me. Thank You that Your supernatural life flows in and through me. I decree and declare that I am a conduit of divine activity. The world around me is shifted and molded by Your love operating through me. I have the victory in every area of my life. In Jesus's name, amen!

 IF YOU HAVE ACCEPTED JESUS CHRIST AS YOUR LORD AND SAVIOR BY FAITH, YOU ARE IN FACT A NEW CREATION! NOW IT IS TIME FOR YOU TO START WALKING LIKE IT.

MORE THAN RELIGION

CHAPTER THEME

Being a Christian—a believer in Jesus Christ—is not a religion. There's a profound difference between religion and a relationship with Jesus. Religion is mankind's attempt to "package" God and His ways into a system that can be replicated and executed. Being a Christian, on the other hand, means being a follower and imitator of Christ—it's a matter of identity, not ritual. It's a dynamic relationship with a living Jesus that changes every part of our lives.

QUESTIONS FOR REFLECTION

1. When was the last time you thought of yourself as an imitator of Jesus?

2. In the time of the early church, nonbelievers began calling Jesus's followers "Christians" because something about the believers reminded the nonbelievers of Jesus Christ. Would nonbelievers today think the same of you? Why or why not?

3. The "Second Great Awakening" furthered God's kingdom significantly. Will you be a part of the next, even greater awakening? Why or why not?

4. How might you be trying to live your Christian life in a "religious" way?

EXPLORING PRINCIPLES AND PURPOSES

1. Define the word *religion.* (p. 35)

    _____

2. What are two meanings for the word *Christian?* (p. 36)

    _____

3. According to Acts 11:26, where were Jesus's disciples first referred to as "Christians"? (p. 37)

    _____

4. As we reflect Jesus, we become "_____ _____." (p. 37)

5. Being a Christian is a matter of _____, not _____. (p. 37)

6. In Galatians 2:20, by what does Paul say he now lives? (p. 37)

    _____

7. What is a "simple but life-changing concept" we need to grasp? (p. 38)

    _____

8. In Old Testament times, where did God often manifest His presence? (p. 38)

    _____

9. Following Jesus's resurrection, where has God dwelled? (p. 38)

    _____

10. By what name do we call the revival in American church culture that took place in the early 1800s? (p. 38)

_____

11. What did the revival of the early 1800s emphasize? (p. 39)

_____

12. What simple truth does the church consistently omit from its teachings and practice? (p. 39)

_____

13. Being a Christian is not for "_____ _____," but for people who have _____, people who have been _____, people who need to be _____. (p. 39)

14. On what basis should we be relating to our heavenly Father? (p. 39)

_____

15. What happens when we yield ourselves to the living, all-powerful person of Jesus? (p. 40)

_____

16. What will happen when the world sees Jesus for who He really is? (p. 40)

_____

17. Why is there a strong temptation among people to be religious? (p. 40)

_____

18. Religion is about "_____ _____," not about _____ _____. (p. 40)

19. What is one way followers of Jesus differ from followers of other religions? (p. 41)

_____

_____

20. Jesus did not come to make us _____. He came to make us _____! (p. 42)

CONCLUSION

Religion doesn't give people life; it essentially kills them by leading them away from the true God or presenting expectations they can never live up to. But Jesus came to make us alive! When we receive and follow Jesus, we have the very life of God operating within us. The moment we accept this simple truth, we enter into a new reality—a reality of victory.

APPLYING PRINCIPLES OF THE SUPERNATURAL

THINKING IT OVER

1. Consider these "Unlocking the Code of the Supernatural Insights" questions from page 43 of *Unlocking the Code of the Supernatural*:

    + What are some characteristics of religion?

    + How does our new life in Christ differ from religion?

    + What does Galatians 2:20 teach us about how we are meant to live our lives in Christ?

    + Where does performance-based religion lead us?

2. What does it mean to you that believers in Jesus are "crucified with Christ"?

ACTING ON IT

1. Make a list of different ways in which you reflect your parents and other family members. Then, make a list of ways in which you reflect Jesus.

2. Take some time each morning to consider what Jesus has done for you.

3. Are you tempted to be religious—to try to earn points in God's kingdom by performing the right way? Pray that God would help you to shed this prideful way of thinking and show you how to better imitate Jesus instead.

PRAYING ABOUT IT

Father, I thank You that Your Word is the final authority in my life. I acknowledge the truth that You are alive within me. I thank You that my righteousness is not based on religious works, but instead on what Jesus Christ accomplished in His death and resurrection. I confess that Jesus is the Lord of my life. All of my validation, worth, and acceptance comes from Him. From this day forward, I walk in the power of the Holy Spirit. I am not controlled by religion, but I am free to serve You in truth. In Jesus's name, amen!

MIRACLE TESTIMONY

SUPERNATURALLY SAVED FROM DEATH

A family friend who lives in Africa was walking on the side of the road in the northern part of his country, which is heavily populated by radical Muslims. The Muslims had been on a campaign of violence for many months. They were terrorizing villages, killing women and children and burning homes to ashes while the inhabitants were still inside. As this man walked along, he witnessed Christians being impaled. Before he could run the other way, the Muslims caught him and held him down so they could pierce him with a rod. Under his breath, the man called on Jesus. There was a sudden blast from heaven that sounded like a trumpet. Apparently, this was a language that only the Muslims could understand because they immediately threw down their rods and ran away. The man's life was supernaturally saved. Jesus is not merely a storybook character. He is alive and all-powerful—and He lives in you.

 JESUS DID NOT COME TO MAKE US RELIGIOUS. HE CAME TO MAKE US ALIVE!

YOU MUST BE BORN AGAIN!

CHAPTER THEME

The modern church strives to be relevant, approachable, and inoffensive. But it often neglects to empower people with the Word of God and teach them what it means to be a new creation in Christ. Many Christians today place great emphasis on looking the part of a Christian, and little emphasis on truly being born again. As a result, they still live defeated lives. In order to understand the fullness of what the Father has given us and to experience His supernatural kingdom, we must recognize and embrace our identity as children of God who have undergone a spiritual rebirth.

QUESTIONS FOR REFLECTION

1. What does being born again mean to you?

2. What religious motions do you find yourself going through?

3. How does knowing that you are one spirit with God change your perspective of your relationship with Him?

4. When the Samaritan woman found herself forever changed by the power of God, she confidently led others to the living water she had found. Are you leading others to Jesus with the same enthusiasm and confidence?

EXPLORING PRINCIPLES AND PURPOSES

1. What was the goal of the "seeker-friendly" movement that emerged in the American church in the early 1990s? (p. 45)

   _____

2. We live in an age when many people place great emphasis on _____ _____ _____ of a Christian, and little emphasis on _____ _____ _____ _____. (p. 46)

3. What is one reason we are not seeing the impact on the world around us that we saw in the early church, despite the great numbers of people who identify themselves as Christians? (p. 46)

   _____

4. Who was Nicodemus and what did he acknowledge about Jesus? (p. 46)

   _____

5. Unless someone is "_____ _____" (John 3:3), that person cannot see the kingdom of God. (p. 46)

6. *"Except a man be born of _____ and of the _____, he cannot enter into the kingdom of God"* (John 3:5). (p. 47)

7. What is the meaning of the Greek word *gennao*, translated *"born"* in John 3:5–6? (p. 47)

   _____

8. What is the translation of the Greek word *kai* that Jesus used in His reply to Nicodemus? (p. 47)

   _____

9. In order to qualify for God's kingdom, you must have a _____ _____. (p. 47)

10. What happens the instant we accept the salvation and lordship of Jesus Christ by faith? (p. 48)

    _____

11. Our physical birth made us _____ in nature, but our spiritual rebirth makes us

    _____ in nature. (p. 48)

12. What is the definition of an individual's nature? (p. 48)

    _____

    _____

13. According to John 1:12–13, what did Jesus give to those who believe on His name? (p. 48)

    _____

14. What is the meaning of the Greek word *ginomai*? What are two English translations of this word?
    (p. 48)

    _____

15. What we often call a "conviction" of wrongdoing is essentially what? (p. 50)

    _____

16. What are a few things that happen when our inner man is in perfect fellowship and alignment with
    our heavenly Father? (p. 50)

    _____

    _____

17. What did Jesus say in John 10:30 that made the Pharisees want to stone Him? (p. 50)

    _____

18. We are one with the Father because we are _____ _____ _____, and Christ is _____ _____ _____ _____. (p. 51)

19. Satan draws his power from _____, _____, and _____. (p. 52)

20. From where do we, as Christians, draw our power and authority? (p. 52)

   _____

21. What was the solution to the Samaritan woman's deepest needs? (p. 52)

   _____

22. *"God is a Spirit: and they that worship Him must worship Him _____ _____ and _____ _____"* (John 4:24). (p. 52)

CONCLUSION

As born-again children of God, new life flows within us, and new life flows from us. When we accept Christ into our spirits, we become filled with God's life-giving presence. We must be born again by God's Spirit so that we can walk as the Spirit-breathed sons and daughters we were destined to be. When we know who we are in God, our whole spiritual paradigm shifts.

APPLYING PRINCIPLES OF THE SUPERNATURAL

THINKING IT OVER

1. Consider these "Unlocking the Code of the Supernatural Insights" questions from page 54 of *Unlocking the Code of the Supernatural*:

   + Name some problems with the "seeker-friendly" approach of the modern church.

   + What ultimately determines our nature?

   + What does a born-again spirit continually desire?

   + What does it mean to be one with the Father?

2. Contrary to the Word of God, what excuses from your thinking and vocabulary are causing your life to remain far below what it is meant to be?

ACTING ON IT

1. Do you ever struggle to grasp what it means to be born again? Spend some time studying God's Word and praying for greater understanding of your new nature in Christ.

2. Do you feel a sense of fear, guilt, and unworthiness that keeps you distant from God? Ask God to take away those feelings of inadequacy and replace them with a strong conviction of your identity as His precious child.

PRAYING ABOUT IT

Father, in the name of Jesus Christ, I thank You for who You are and all that You have done for me. Today, I accept the truth that I am one spirit with You. According to John 10:30 and John 17:21, I am one with Jesus, as He is one with the Father. Right now, I submit myself to the lordship of Christ. I declare that I am born again of incorruptible seed. The Holy Spirit has given me spiritual birth, and I have Your DNA within my being. Thank You, Father, for revealing this mystery to me! In Jesus's name, amen!

 GOD NEITHER WANTS TO BEAT YOU DOWN WITH RELIGION NOR STROKE YOUR EXISTENTIAL EGO. HE SIMPLY WANTS YOU TO KNOW WHO YOU ARE IN HIM.

CONSEQUENCES OF THE RELIGIOUS SPIRIT

CHAPTER THEME

Believers frequently find it difficult to distinguish between a man-made religious system and a God-ordained relationship. The apostle James calls us to practice *"pure religion"* (James 1:27)—to exercise spiritual disciplines from the right motives grounded in love for God. What does pure religion look like? It encompasses self-control, care for the vulnerable, and turning away from the world's ways of thinking. Unless our religion is characterized by these three things, it is vain religion that only produces spiritual barrenness.

QUESTIONS FOR REFLECTION

1. In what ways are you performing for God rather than loving Him?

2. Do you have the qualities of someone who practices "pure religion"?

3. How responsive are you to God's Word and Spirit?

4. Would you consider yourself a "resilient disciple" such as those who were identified in the Barna study? Why or why not?

EXPLORING PRINCIPLES AND PURPOSES

1. In what way does James use the term *"religion"* in James 1:26? (p. 56)

    _____

2. Define the term "pure." (p. 56)

    _____

    _____

3. To practice pure religion is to exercise _____ _____ from the

    _____ _____. (p. 56)

4. What is the first quality of those who practice pure religion? (p. 56)

    _____

5. According to James 1:27, those who practice pure religion must actively care for "_____

    _____ and _____." (p. 57)

6. What is the meaning of the Greek word *aspilos* (*"unspotted"*) in James 1:27? (p. 57)

    _____

7. What is the meaning of the Greek word *mataios* (*"vain"*) in James 1:26? (p. 57)

    _____

8. A religious spirit may stem from a _____, _____ _____ or a

    _____ _____—or both. (p. 58)

9.   What are a few ways a religious spirit affects people? (p. 58)

_____

_____

10. What is one meaning of the Greek word *eusebeia* ("*godliness*") in 2 Timothy 3:5? (p. 58)

_____

11. What Greek word refers to explosive power? (p. 58)

_____

12. The religious spirit encourages people to sound like _____ but not *be*
     _____. (p. 60)

13. According to a Barna study, what percent of young adults with a Christian background are "resilient disciples"? (p. 60)

_____

14. When Jesus cursed the fig tree in Mark 11, He was not cursing the natural tree itself. What was He actually cursing? (p. 61)

_____

15. In Genesis 3:7, what do the fig leaves symbolize? (p. 62)

_____

16. What is the first attribute of the fig tree that Jesus cursed? (p. 62)

_____

17. Our union with Jesus Christ is supposed to produce _____ _____.
     (p. 63)

18. When is spiritual fruit produced in the lives of believers? (p. 63)

_____

19. What English word derives from the Greek term *hypokrites?* (p. 64)

_____

20. Hypocrisy opens the door to _____—of ourselves and others. (p. 65)

21. According to James 1:22, what will cause us to become deceived? (p. 65)

_____

22. What meanings does the Greek word *epilanthanomai* ("*forgets*") hold? (p. 66)

_____

23. The religious spirit produces only _____, _____, and _____. (p. 66)

CONCLUSION

We must not allow ourselves to become ensnared by the spirit of religion—performing religious rituals without experiencing the newness and freedom that come with being a believer in Christ. When we embrace an outward form of religion, our lives will be characterized by barrenness, hypocrisy, and deception. We can become bound by the spirit of deception without even knowing it. The Word of God alone has the power to break the strongholds of religion, barrenness, hypocrisy, and deception. God wants to show us a better way to live in His kingdom. We can live fruitful, abundant lives that prompt the world around us to want to know Jesus more each day!

THINKING IT OVER

1. Consider these "Unlocking the Code of the Supernatural Insights" questions from pages 67 and 68 of *Unlocking the Code of the Supernatural*:

   * What are the qualifications of someone who demonstrates *"pure religion,"* as described in James 1:26–27?

   * Describe the three characteristics of the spirit of religion as illustrated by the fig tree Jesus cursed.

   * What does it mean to have *"a form of godliness, but denying the power thereof"* (2 Timothy 3:5)?

   * What has the power to break the strongholds of religion, barrenness, hypocrisy, and deception in our lives?

2. If someone were to ask you whether you have a relationship with God, how would you respond?

ACTING ON IT

1. Which characteristic of "pure religion" do you most struggle with manifesting? Pray that God would transform this area of your life. Then make a list of action steps you could take to better exhibit that characteristic.

2. Can you think of anyone in your life who has *"a form of godliness, but* [denies] *the power thereof"*? Pray that God would draw this person close to Him and show them their need for a genuine, supernatural relationship with Him.

3. Are you wearing any religious "masks"? Ask God to remove any such masks from your life and to help you live according to your true nature and identity in Him.

PRAYING ABOUT IT

Heavenly Father, I thank You that, as a new creation, I am free from the religious spirit and its consequences. I am not just a hearer of the Word but also a doer of the Word. Rather than having merely a form of godliness, I have the explosive, supernatural power that accompanies true godliness, transforming me and those around me. Because I have been made new in Christ, I practice true religion—exercising self-control, reaching out to those in need, and keeping myself unspotted from the world. In Jesus's name, amen!

BREAKING THE SHACKLES OF RELIGIOSITY

A dear sister in our church shared about how she used to live a sinful lifestyle full of witchcraft, rebellion, immorality, and hatred for God. She had grown up in Catholicism, and, due to her background in religion and church tradition, she'd never had a personal relationship with the Lord. And so, she found herself in that dark place.

Nevertheless, she desired to get closer to God at some point in her life. One day, she decided to go on a fast, during which she literally heard the voice of God prompting her to surrender her life to Christ. She prayed a prayer of salvation, and, several days later, she was baptized in the Holy Spirit at our church. Since then, this sister has ministered to many people, including her loved ones, who have come to salvation. She is bearing good fruit! It all began when she broke the shackles of the religious spirit and experienced a personal relationship with Jesus.

 WE CAN LIVE FRUITFUL, ABUNDANT LIVES THAT PROMPT THE WORLD AROUND US TO WANT TO KNOW JESUS MORE EACH DAY!

BREAKING THE CYCLE OF STRIVING

CHAPTER THEME

The apostle Paul wrote to Galatian believers who had begun striving for their salvation rather than allowing the Holy Spirit to lead them. They had fallen into a cycle of religious bondage—a form of bondage in which many believers today find themselves trapped. When we strive to please God, we are not able to obey Him as we should, and our relationship with the Lord becomes unfruitful. God's kingdom was never meant to be manifested through human effort. Christ has already accomplished the work for us. All we need to do is respond to His grace.

QUESTIONS FOR REFLECTION

1. Have you been making any requirements for salvation—either for yourself or others—that go beyond the gospel of Jesus Christ?

2. In what ways are you striving to earn God's love?

3. Are you trying to connect with God through your works rather than by His Spirit?

4. What does it mean to you that you are free from the bondage of striving to earn God's love?

EXPLORING PRINCIPLES AND PURPOSES

1. Who were the "Judaizers" and what did they teach? (p. 69)

    _____

2. Judaizers were living according to _____ _____ instead of _____. (p. 70)

3. Into what were the Galatian believers thrust as a result of the Judaizers' teaching? (p. 70)

    _____

4. What are two meanings of the Greek term *baskaino* ("*bewitched*") in Galatians 3:1? (p. 70)

    _____ _____

5. To what can we compare religion without a relationship with God? (p. 71)

    _____

6. What were some erroneous behaviors Peter was guilty of committing? (pp. 71–72)

    _____

    _____

7. Define the word *strive*. (p. 72)

    _____

    _____

8. What truth is Paul referring to in Galatians 3:1? (p. 72)

    _____

9. God wanted the Galatian believers to respond to His _____, not to

    _____ for His acceptance. (p. 72)

10. Spiritual perfection can only come about through the _____ _____. (p. 73)

11. What does *"flesh"* refer to in Roman 8:8? (p. 73)

_____

12. When do our works become misplaced? (p. 73)

_____

_____

13. What is the meaning of the Greek word *steko* (*"stand fast"*) in Galatians 5:1? (p. 74)

_____

14. The command to *"stand fast"* implies that our freedom in Christ is a _____

_____, a _____ _____. (p. 74)

15. What forces attempt to move us away from our standing in Christ? (p. 74)

_____

16. What is a second remedy for religious oppression? (p. 74)

_____

17. What happens when we are not confident that we have been justified by faith and that God loves us? (p. 75)

_____

18. What are a few things Christians do to attempt to look "spiritual"? (p. 75)

_____

_____

19. We were not created to _____ for God, but simply to _____ Him. (p. 75)

20. How has God already proven that He loves you? (pp. 75–76)

    _____

    _____

21. We are _____ to the law, and as a result, we are _____ to sin! (p. 76)

22. Why do we keep God's commands? (p. 76)

    _____

CONCLUSION

God loves you! This is the simple truth that will radically reshape your life. We can never perform enough to cover up our spiritual nakedness. And if we are believers, we don't need to—because we have already been covered by the blood of Jesus. We have been delivered from the bondage of striving to earn God's love. We are now free to walk in the Spirit—to stand fast in our secure position in Christ and to live according to the love and grace of God. There is no greater way to live a life of victory than to walk according to the Spirit of God.

APPLYING PRINCIPLES OF THE SUPERNATURAL

THINKING IT OVER

1. Consider these "Unlocking the Code of the Supernatural Insights" questions from pages 77 and 78 of *Unlocking the Code of the Supernatural*:

   + What happens in our relationship with God the more religious we are?

   + In Galatians 2, for what reason did Paul need to rebuke Peter?

   + How do we attain spiritual perfection?

   + What does it mean to walk in the Spirit?

2. How will you "stand fast" in the truth that your freedom in Christ is a finished work, a spiritual reality?

ACTING ON IT

1. Can you think of anyone who has "bewitched" you, a family member, or a friend into a legalistic outlook? Pray that God would free you and others from the bondage of legalism. Then, take steps to gently correct the person who is emphasizing striving rather than grace.

2. Make a list of ways you are involved in your church or ministry. Then, take some time to prayerfully consider your motives for participating in these programs and activities. Pray that God would orient your involvement to come from a place of love and desire to serve, rather than a position of earning His love.

PRAYING ABOUT IT

Father, in the name of Jesus Christ, I declare that I will no longer be bound by a vicious cycle of striving to obtain Your love and acceptance. I stand fast in the liberty with which Christ has made me free. I rest in the finished work of Jesus. Your truth is the only truth that matters in my life. I reject the lie that tells me Your grace is somehow insufficient for me. Thank You for my freedom, wholeness, and victory in Christ. In Jesus's name, amen!

 THERE IS NO GREATER WAY TO LIVE A LIFE OF VICTORY THAN TO WALK ACCORDING TO THE SPIRIT OF GOD.

FREEDOM FROM THE LAW

CHAPTER THEME

In the book of Romans, Paul draws a stark distinction between law and grace, comparing the law to marriage under the Mosaic law in which a woman was bound to her husband for the duration of his life but was free to marry another man if her husband died. Through His death and resurrection, Christ has freed us from our bondage to the law and given us the legal right to be married to Him. Yet many Christians today are guilty of spiritual adultery: they are trying to simultaneously be married to the law and to Christ. This is a recipe for frustration and spiritual barrenness. When we are freed from the law, we are empowered to *"serve [God] in newness of spirit"* (Romans 7:6).

QUESTIONS FOR REFLECTION

1. In what ways might you be trying to live according to law and grace at the same time?

2. Have you ever had an experience in which you were tempted to do the opposite of what the law says? How did you act in that circumstance?

3. How do you feel after you have sinned? What is the first thing you do?

4. In what ways might you be a more effective Christian if you were to cast off a sense of condemnation and instead trust in and receive God's love and mercy?

EXPLORING PRINCIPLES AND PURPOSES

1. In the book of Romans, what theme does the apostle Paul focus on? (p. 79)

   _____

2. Under the Mosaic law, how long was a woman bound to her husband? (p. 80)

   _____

3. To what were people bound before Christ came? (p. 80)

   _____

4. Romans 7:4 says that we are *"dead to the law by* _____ _____ _____ _____." (p. 80)

5. When were we freed from the law? (p. 80)

   _____

6. When we were married to the law, we were impregnated with _____, _____, _____, and _____, which ultimately produced death. (p. 80)

7. With what are we impregnated when we give our lives to Christ? (p. 80)

   _____

8. What is the evidence that we are still married to the law? (p. 82)

   _____

9. To what does the Greek word *palaiotes* ("*oldness*") refer? (p. 82)

   _____

10. What is the meaning of the Greek word *gramma* ("*letter*")? (p. 82)

   _____

11. At what point did the human race enter into spiritual debt? (p. 82)

   _____

12. The reason God gave the law to the Israelites in the wilderness was to show them what? (p. 82)

   _____

13. The law is a _____ _____ that reveals to us our unrighteousness apart from God. (p. 82)

14. What is the meaning of the Greek word *epignosis* ("*knowledge*") in Romans 3:20? (p. 83)

   _____

15. What is the dictionary definition of the term *condemn,* and how does it compare to the meaning of the Greek word *katakrima* ("*condemnation*") in Romans 8:1? (p. 84)

   _____

   _____

16. Condemnation is an overwhelming feeling of _____ that prohibits us from receiving God's _____ and _____. (p. 84)

17. What allows Satan to manipulate and control us? (p. 84)

   _____

18. The truth is that there is _____ _____ to those who are in Christ Jesus. (p. 84)

19. In Genesis 3:8, what did Adam and Eve do after they sinned? (p. 85)

_____

CONCLUSION

The law is a magnifying glass that reveals to us our unrighteousness apart from God. As believers, we have been freed from the law and are empowered to live a life that is victorious in every area. Despite our freedom from the law, too many of us continue to feel condemned by our sin, even after we have repented of it. This keeps us stuck in a state of spiritual, emotional, and even physical stagnation. The truth is that there is *no condemnation* to those who are in Christ Jesus. God's plan for you is so much greater than your failure or your sin. Jesus Christ took your death sentence on Himself so that you could live abundantly. Jesus's blood is fully sufficient to cover your sin and shame. When you understand this truth, you will approach God confidently as your Father and Deliverer.

APPLYING PRINCIPLES OF THE SUPERNATURAL

THINKING IT OVER

1. Consider these "Unlocking the Code of the Supernatural Insights" questions from pages 86 and 87 of *Unlocking the Code of the Supernatural*:

    + What does it mean to be married to the law? What does it mean to be married to Christ?

    + In Romans 7:6, what does *kainotes*, the Greek word translated *"newness,"* signify?

    + What evidence shows that we are still living as if we are married to the law?

    + What lie from Satan keeps many believers under a sense of condemnation? What is the answer to this lie?

2. What lies has Satan been telling you? How will you respond to them?

ACTING ON IT

1. Are you giving Satan control over you by living with a sense of condemnation? Pray today that God would help you to recognize your worth as His child and to receive His love and mercy.

2. Are you running away from the Lord rather than running toward Him? Make a list of the sins in your life that are making you feel unworthy of going to God and being used by Him. Then pray over the list, asking God to forgive you, to cleanse you, and to free you from bondage.

PRAYING ABOUT IT

Father, in the name of Your Son Jesus Christ, I declare that I am free from the law. I live under the abundant flow of Your grace, which empowers me to live righteously. I take authority over Satan and all of his wicked devices in the form of guilt, shame, and condemnation. I loose myself from the bondage of condemnation right now, and I declare that the person whom the Son sets free is free indeed. I will no longer strive for Your love and acceptance, but I will receive the fullness of Your redemption in every area of my life. In the precious name of Jesus Christ, amen!

 JESUS'S BLOOD IS TRULY SUFFICIENT TO COVER YOUR SIN AND SHAME. WHEN YOU UNDERSTAND THIS TRUTH, YOU WILL APPROACH GOD CONFIDENTLY AS YOUR FATHER AND DELIVERER.

PUTTING ON CHRIST AS OUR RIGHTEOUSNESS

CHAPTER THEME

The law is a powerful stronghold that prevents many believers from progressing in their walks with God. Believers strive to become righteous on the basis of their own efforts. But righteousness is not something we can earn or achieve; it is a position—a seat of acceptance, favor, and blessing in our relationship with the Lord. Jesus Christ paid the price for our righteousness with His precious blood. God wants you to exchange your righteousness for Christ's righteousness.

QUESTIONS FOR REFLECTION

1. How would you define *righteousness*? What is the basis of a Christian's righteousness?

2. What is keeping you from sitting down in the seat of favor, love, and authority that God has provided for you?

3. When you were growing up, did you feel you needed to compete for love, acceptance, and recognition? If so, how has this upbringing affected your relationship with God?

4. In what ways might you be trying to do "penance" for your sins and mistakes rather than receiving God's forgiveness for them and accepting your righteousness in Christ?

EXPLORING PRINCIPLES AND PURPOSES

1. What Greek word is rendered as *"knowledge"* in Romans 10:2, and where else in Romans can we find this word? (p. 89)

    _____

2. Based on Romans 10:3, of what two things were the Israelites ignorant? (p. 90)

    _____

3. Being righteous isn't a matter of doing _____ _____ but rather of _____ _____. (p. 90)

4. What happens when we fall out of our spiritual position? (p. 90)

    _____

5. Righteousness is a seat of _____, _____, and _____ in our relationship with the Lord. (p. 90)

6. Complete this verse: *"For Christ is* _____ _____ ____ _____ _____ _____ _____ *to every one that believes"* (Romans 10:4). (p. 90)

7. What tremendous price was paid to reserve your seat of righteousness? (p. 91)

    _____

8. God wants you to exchange _____ righteousness for _____ righteousness. (p. 91)

9. What has the power to bring us eternal salvation and the indwelling Holy Spirit to live a supernatural life? (p. 92)

    _____

10. The _____ _____ _____ is the answer to the perils that plague our world and our church. (p. 92)

11. What imparts God's righteousness to us? (p. 92)

   _____

12. Christ was *made...to be sin* (2 Corinthians 5:21) on our behalf. What happened when He was crucified? (p. 93)

   _____

13. What are two meanings of the Greek term *ginomai* ("made") in 2 Corinthians 5:21? (p. 94)

   _____

14. At what point did God supernaturally cause us to be just like Him in nature and spiritual identity? (p. 94)

   _____

15. In ancient Hebrew culture, who received a special blessing from the father, and what was the significance of this blessing? (p. 95)

   _____

16. In Genesis 25, who received the blessing of the firstborn: Jacob or Esau? Who should have received the blessing of the firstborn according to Hebrew custom? (p. 95)

   _____

17. In what way did Jacob "put on" his elder brother, Esau? (p. 96)

   _____

18. What is the literal meaning of the Greek term *endyo* ("*put you on*") in Romans 13:14? (p. 96)

_____

19. Jesus Christ is our _____ _____ in redemption. (p. 97)

CONCLUSION

The moment we gave ourselves to Jesus Christ, God supernaturally caused us to be like Him in nature and spiritual identity. Just as Jacob put on the best garments of his elder brother, Esau, and received the blessing, we "put on" Jesus's best garments—His righteousness—when we gave our life to Him. Our clothing of human works is not sufficient to position us to be eternally blessed by God. By faith, we clothe ourselves with Jesus Christ and "sink into" His righteousness.

APPLYING PRINCIPLES OF THE SUPERNATURAL

THINKING IT OVER

1. Consider these "Unlocking the Code of the Supernatural Insights" questions from page 98 of *Unlocking the Code of the Supernatural*:

    + What is the biblical definition of *righteousness*?

    + Why is the gospel so powerful, as Paul writes about in Romans 1:16–17?

    + What is the difference between the idea of "becoming" righteous and being "made" righteous?

    + What inheritance have we been given in Christ?

2. How might you live differently now that you understand that you are "wearing" the life of the Lord Jesus Christ?

ACTING ON IT

1. Make a list of some of the privileges that come from being a joint-heir with Christ. Take time to praise God today for granting you this new identity.

2. As you are getting dressed each morning this week, use the change of clothing as a reminder that, when you accepted Jesus as your Savior, you put on Christ. Take a moment to pray that God would guide you in "sinking into" His righteousness that day.

Heavenly Father, thank You that You call me to draw near to You in intimate fellowship on the basis of Christ's righteousness. I have been brought near to You through the precious blood of Your Son. By faith, I clothe myself with Jesus Christ, my Elder Brother. I walk in His character, nature, and authority, wearing His righteousness, not my own. Thank You that I am a joint-heir with Jesus and have been given unlimited access to Your blessings. I enter into the victory of this reality. In Jesus's name, amen!

 HOW CAN SIN, SHAME, AND CONDEMNATION CONTROL US WHEN WE ARE WALKING IN THE CHARACTER, NATURE, AND AUTHORITY OF JESUS, OUR ELDER BROTHER?

PART II:
LIVING A SUPERNATURAL LIFESTYLE

CREATION VERSUS REFORMATION

CHAPTER THEME

The Reformation of the fifteenth century corrected many religious errors and abuses in the church, but it also led to an emphasis on reformation rather than recreation. Many churches today focus their efforts on reforming people externally rather than helping them understand what it means to be a new creation, which has led to a performance-based culture in many sectors of Christianity. Christians need more than just various reforms; we are to experience radical, supernatural transformation of spirit, soul, and body. When we live according to our recreation in God's image, we will not be able to retreat back into our old life.

QUESTIONS FOR REFLECTION

1. How would you like to be filled with God's Spirit in such a powerful way that you and other believers literally alter the fabric of the culture in which you live?

2. Have you ever imagined doing the same things the apostles in the book of Acts did through the power of the Holy Spirit? How can you inspire other Christians to embrace their supernatural calling rather than settling for "church-as-usual"?

3. How do you feel when you consider what the world will look like after the *supernatural recreation* takes place?

4. What does it mean for you to be the salt of the earth and the light of world?

EXPLORING PRINCIPLES AND PURPOSES

1. Whose conversion and subsequent actions led to Christianity becoming the state religion of Rome in the year 380? (p. 101)

   _____

2. The Reformation led to the development of what three things? (p. 102)

   _____

3. What did the Catholic Church undergo as a result of the upheaval caused by the Reformation? (p. 102)

   _____

4. What is the definition of *reformation?* (p. 102)

   _____

5. What is one negative result of the Reformation and Counter-Reformation? (p. 102)

   _____

6. What do many churches today focus their time, money, and energy on? What should they focus on instead? (p. 103)

   _____

7. Complete this verse: *"And have put on the new man, which is _____ ____ _____ after the image of Him that created him"* (Colossians 3:10). (p. 104)

8. When God recreates you, He is the _____ of the city called "___ _____ _____." (p. 104)

9. What rights does a founder of a city have? (p. 104)

    _____

10. God is not calling us to change our ecclesiastical institutions, structures, and practices. What is He calling us to undergo instead? (p. 105)

    _____

11. Why are many people trapped in "church-as-usual"? (p. 105)

    _____

    _____

12. God wants us to be His _____ and _____ of the new covenant. (p. 105)

13. The church may have been _____, but it has not been fully _____. (p. 105)

14. Believers were never created for church-as-usual. We were created for the _____! (p. 106)

15. Instead of *revival* or *reformation*, what could the next end-time move of God be called? (p. 106)

    _____

16. In Matthew 5:13 and 14, how does Jesus describe believers? (p. 107)

    _____

17. You were created to be a _____ to God's _____

_____. (p. 107)

CONCLUSION

Believers in Christ desire more than just church-as-usual. We desire more than just external reform. We desire recreation. When we are recreated, we are like a new city founded by God, where His government has been established. Christians who are recreated in God's very image do not find it difficult to love others. They are completely sold out for Jesus Christ. They no longer undergo spiritual wilderness experiences. It is time to enter into the fullness of what God has to offer. You were created for God's glory and power to be manifested through you.

APPLYING PRINCIPLES OF THE SUPERNATURAL

THINKING IT OVER

1. Consider these "Unlocking the Code of the Supernatural Insights" questions from page 108 of *Unlocking the Code of the Supernatural*:

    + Why did the Protestant Reformation take place?

    + What was a major drawback of the Reformation?

    + What does the Greek word *ktizo*, translated as *"created"* in Colossians 3:10, reveal about what it means for us to be made new by God?

    + What will the next end-time move of God be like?

2. What would our world look like if today's Christians *"turned the world upside down"* (Acts 17:6) like the early believers did?

ACTING ON IT

1. Consider what negative behaviors in your life you may have been trying to "reform." Then, pray that God would not just reform you but recreate you in His image.

2. Read Matthew 5:13–14 and think about what it means to be *"the salt of the earth"* and *"the light of the world."* Make a list of steps you and other believers can take to become salt and light in your community, and then follow through with them.

Father, in the name of Jesus, I recognize that I am recreated in the image of Christ Jesus and that, by design, I am called and commissioned to carry Your supernatural power. Thank You for including me in the end-time move of the Spirit to bring the revelation of who You are to others around me. Right now, I receive a supernatural download of new-creation power, which will enable me to think like You, speak like You, and operate like You! I will no longer settle for church-as-usual, but I will absorb the reality of Your kingdom into every area of my life. Thank You for releasing Your supernatural power through me!

MIRACLE TESTIMONY

AN ANGELIC VISITATION

One night, I had an angelic visitation. I awoke from sleep and saw an angel staring at me with the most perplexed look on his face. It was as if he was bewildered by the notion that God would spend such effort and resources on "little ol' me." The angel didn't say anything; he just kept gazing. However, it was as if we were having a full conversation. The word that came to mind was *rest*. At that time, I was very discouraged by the persecution I had been experiencing from other believers. I was encouraged by this encounter, and, when I woke up the next day, I had fresh zeal and enthusiasm for the things of God.

 WE WILL SHOW THE WORLD HOW REAL GOD IS BY LIVING AS THE NEW CREATIONS IN CHRIST THAT HE HAS MADE US TO BE.

WILL YOU BE MADE WHOLE?

CHAPTER THEME

Many believers are in a state of spiritual and physical infirmity. Like the man at the Pool of Bethesda in John 5, they are waiting for God to change their circumstances. But God has already given us everything we need as new creations to live the life that He has ordained for us. Jesus asks us, as He did the man at the pool, "Will you be made whole?" Then, He calls us to rise, take up our beds, and walk!

QUESTIONS FOR REFLECTION

1. When have you considered yourself a victim and waited on other people to change your circumstances?

2. How do you respond to Jesus's question, "Will you be made whole?"

3. In John 5, the man's *"bed"* (*krabattos*) was a symbol of his affliction and was part of his identity. What parts of your identity is Jesus calling you to take ownership of and actively renew?

4. In what ways is your life a witness to Jesus's resurrection power?

EXPLORING PRINCIPLES AND PURPOSES

1. For how long had the man at the Pool of Bethesda been lame? (p. 110)

   _____

2. What happens when we are living beneath the potential God has given us in Christ? (p. 111)

   _____

3. Salvation is more than saying a prayer to accept Jesus Christ, but it involves a holistic deliverance of _____, _____, and _____. (p. 111)

4. What question does Jesus ask the man at the Pool of Bethesda? (p. 111)

   _____

5. Living in victory involves our _____. (p. 111)

6. On what was the man at the pool's wholeness contingent? (p. 112)

   _____

7. In John 5:8, Jesus commands the man, "_____, _____ _____ _____ _____, and _____." (p. 112)

8. To what dimension of our triune being does the command *Rise* correspond? (p. 112)

   _____

9. What is the meaning of the Greek word *egeiro* ("*rise*") in John 5:8? (p. 112)

   _____

10. From what was Jesus awakening the man when He called him to rise? (p. 112)

   _____

11. The Word of God contains _____-_____ _____. (p. 113)

12. When we gave our hearts to Jesus, our spiritual DNA was changed from _____ to _____, from _____ to _____. (p. 114)

13. To what dimension of our triune being does the command *"Take up your bed"* correspond? (p. 114)

_____

14. What meanings does the Greek word *airo* ("take up") in John 5:8 hold? (p. 114)

_____

15. The man at the pool's participation in Jesus's command represents _____ in the life of the believer. (p. 114)

16. Sanctification is the process of _____ something for holy purposes. (p. 114)

17. What is the Greek word for "sanctification"? What is another common translation for this word in the King James Version? (p. 114)

_____

18. What transformation must we undergo in order to fully embrace all that Jesus has accomplished for us? (p. 115)

_____

19. Sanctification is not just behavioral modification. It is not following dos and don'ts. What is it? (p. 115)

_____

_____

20. To what dimension of our triune being does the command *"Walk"* correspond? (p. 117)

_____

21. What does the pool in John 5 represent? (p. 117)

_____

22. What is the meaning of the Greek word *peripateo* (*"walk"*) in John 5:8? (p. 117)

_____

CONCLUSION

Being a believer in Jesus is not about being ordinary. We are not to live a life of mediocrity. We are called to live a life pregnant with the supernatural. After we receive Jesus as our Savior, we are to walk as living testaments to the resurrection power of Jesus Christ. Like the man at the Pool of Bethesda in John 5, we have been commissioned by God to walk out His "super" in our natural. He wants us to demonstrate to the fallen world around us that His power is truly omnipotent!

APPLYING PRINCIPLES OF THE SUPERNATURAL

THINKING IT OVER

1. Consider these "Unlocking the Code of the Supernatural Insights" questions from page 120 of *Unlocking the Code of the Supernatural*:

   * What is the spiritual significance of Jesus's command to rise?

   * What does it mean for us to "take up our bed"?

   * Why did Jesus tell the infirm man to walk rather than to step into the Pool of Bethesda?

   * How should we "walk forward" in life as new creations in Christ?

2. What command from God's Word can you act on today?

ACTING ON IT

1. Read John 5. Then, consider situations in the past or present for which you've said, "One day...." Reflect on those situations. Spend some time in prayer telling God you're ready to be made whole and acknowledging His unlimited power and mercy.

2. Consider each of these questions from page 119 of *Unlocking the Code of the Supernatural*:

   + Is my life exemplifying the power that raised Jesus from the dead?

   + Do people receive an impartation of the victorious Spirit of God from me?

   + Are people challenged to live at a higher level of spiritual life because of me?

   + Are people convinced that they can live a life free from sin because of my testimony?

   If your answer to any of these questions is no, pray that God would help you to live in His Spirit as a testament to the power of Christ.

PRAYING ABOUT IT

Father, in the name of Jesus Christ, I recognize that it is Your will for me to be whole in every area of my life. Right now, I receive wholeness in my spirit, soul, and body. I declare that I have been made complete. Today, I decide to renew my mind through the Word of God. Father, please demonstrate Your kingdom through me! I receive supernatural empowerment by Your Spirit to live out Your original intent for my life. I *"mortify the deeds of the body"* through the power of Your indwelling Spirit. Fear, anger, and bitterness no longer control me. In Jesus's name, amen!

 GOD WANTS US TO DEMONSTRATE TO THE FALLEN WORLD AROUND US THAT HIS POWER IS TRULY OMNIPOTENT!

OLD THINGS HAVE PASSED AWAY

CHAPTER THEME

Many believers attempt to embrace their new life but fail to grasp the spiritual reality that, from God's perspective, their old life is no more. They hold on to the guilt, shame, and condemnation of their past negative experiences. They hold themselves hostage to the past. Yet, as born-again children of God, our pasts have been wiped away. We are people who have been redeemed from the old and translated by the Spirit of God into the new.

QUESTIONS FOR REFLECTION

1. Have you been judging yourself for your past mistakes and sins? How does God want you to think about them?

2. How does knowing you are an emissary of God's kingdom challenge the way you think of and speak about your past?

3. What sin in your past will you release today, knowing that God has "cast it into the depths of the sea" and no longer remembers it?

4. What would it look like for you to live a guilt-free life?

EXPLORING PRINCIPLES AND PURPOSES

1. How does Satan use people's memories of negative experiences? (p. 122)

_____

2. What is one reason why it is so difficult for us to accept the fact that, if we are born-again children of God, our pasts have been wiped away? (p. 122)

_____

3. What is the meaning of the Greek word *archaios* (*"old things"*) in 2 Corinthians 5:17? (p. 124)

_____

4. To what does the phrase *"old things"* refer? (p. 124)

_____

5. What is the meaning of the Greek word *parerchomai* (*"passed away"*) in 2 Corinthians 5:17? (p. 124)

_____

6. Our old nature has indeed _____. It has been _____. It is no more! (p. 124)

7. Name a few adjectives the church frequently uses for Christians that effectively resurrect their old nature. (p. 124)

_____

8. Complete this quote from 2 Corinthians 5:20: "*Now then we are* _____ _____ _____, *as though God did beseech you by us: we pray you in Christ's stead, be you reconciled to God.*" (p. 124)

9. What are we called by God to represent? (p. 124)

_____

10. We are _____ of the _____ of the new nature. (p. 124)

11. Why does Satan use the past to attempt to control us? (p. 125)

_____

_____

12. Who paid the price for our guilt and shame and made us free to worship God? (p. 125)

_____

13. God has cast our sins into the _____ of the _____. (pp. 125–126)

14. Complete this verse: *"For I will be _____ to their unrighteousness, and their sins and their iniquities will I _____ no more"* (Hebrews 8:12). (p. 126)

15. What are two purposes of God's grace and mercy? (p. 126)

_____

16. What is a definition of the Greek word *epilanthanomai* (*"forgetting"*) in Philippians 3:13? (pp. 126–127)

_____

17. What lie of Satan do many Christians believe? (p. 127)

_____

18. Our _____ does not determine our _____. (p. 128)

19. What are a few meanings of the Greek word *dioko* ("*press*") in Philippians 1:14? (p. 128)

_____

_____

20. The new covenant God has established with believers is "*established upon* _____

_____." (p. 129)

21. Who is the Mediator of the new covenant? (p. 130)

_____

22. What is the purpose of Yom Kippur or the Day of Atonement? (p. 130)

_____

23. What did the blood on the mercy seat symbolize? (p. 131)

_____

24. Under the new covenant, who is both the sin offering and the scapegoat? (p. 131)

_____

25. Why do we no longer have to follow external rules and regulations? (p. 132)

_____

CONCLUSION

As believers, we must not settle for anything less than a new life in Christ Jesus. We live under a new covenant that exceeds anything we could ever imagine in the natural realm. This new covenant is established upon "*better promises*" (Hebrews 8:6) than the old covenant, which was a continual remembrance of sin. Because of Christ's once-and-for-all sacrifice for our iniquities, we no longer need to have a continual consciousness of sin. We can confess our transgressions to God and immediately receive His forgiveness. He no longer remembers our sins. We are no longer defined by our past. Instead, we are new creations!

THINKING IT OVER

1. Consider these "Unlocking the Code of the Supernatural Insights" questions from pages 132–133 of *Unlocking the Code of the Supernatural*:

   + What does the Bible say God does with our sins when we have sincerely repented of them?

   + What is God's "memory" of our sins?

   + What is the purpose of God's grace and mercy?

   + What is the difference between the old covenant and the new covenant?

2. What "internal tattoos" is Satan using to accuse you and manipulate you into trying to earn God's love, acceptance, and validation?

ACTING ON IT

1. Are you judging another believer because of their past? Pray to the Lord for forgiveness and ask Him to help you see that believer as a redeemed child of God.

2. Make a list of words you've used to describe yourself that evoke your old nature or remind you of sins for which you've been forgiven. Then, tear up that list, praying as you do so that God would remind you that you have been set free from your wretchedness.

PRAYING ABOUT IT

Father, I thank You for the eternal, atoning sacrifice of Your Son Jesus. I thank You that my sins have been washed away and cast into the depths of the sea. From this day forward, I recognize that You no longer remember my past sins. Therefore, I no longer remember my past sins either! I embrace the full magnitude of the new covenant. I live under a better covenant than that of the Old Testament patriarchs. Everywhere I go and every person I meet is an opportunity for me to represent the kingdom of God, and I walk in my assignment as an ambassador of Christ. In the name of Jesus Christ, I pray. Amen!

 YOU ARE NO LONGER YOUR PAST. INSTEAD, YOU ARE A NEW CREATION, AND YOU ARE EVERYTHING GOD SAYS YOU ARE AS HIS BELOVED SON OR DAUGHTER!

LIVING FROM THE INSIDE OUT

CHAPTER THEME

Transformation begins from the inside out, not the outside in. Religion focuses on the outward person, but true Christianity deals with the inner person. Until our inner nature is transformed, we will find it impossible to carry out the purpose and plan of God for our lives. Internal change isn't just possible—it's required. True holiness comes from within us. God wants us to manifest what He has already deposited inside of us. We have to bring it out!

QUESTIONS FOR REFLECTION

1. How might you be trying to live your Christian life from the outside in, rather than the inside out?

2. What comes to your mind when you think of the word *obedience*? How does knowing Christians are wired to obey God affect your perception of the term?

3. What progress are you making on renewing your mind according to God's will? How can you further that progress?

4. Consider the form Jesus took on when He was transfigured, as described in Matthew 17:1–2. How can this account help you begin to see yourself the way God intended?

EXPLORING PRINCIPLES AND PURPOSES

1. Complete this verse: "*A good man out of the good treasure of his heart brings forth* _____ _____*: and an evil man out of the evil treasure brings forth* _____ _____*"* (Matthew 12:35). (p. 134)

2. Of what did the Pharisees accuse Jesus's disciples in the gospel of Mark? (pp. 134–135)

   _____

3. The Pharisees had the right garments, the right education, the right ceremonies, the right speech, and even the right walk, but they were _____ on the inside. (p. 135)

4. On what did the holiness movement focus? (p. 135)

   _____

   _____

5. Although there were positive aspects to this movement, what did an emphasis on external matters lead many people in the movement to do? (p. 136)

   _____

6. What is the meaning of the Greek word *energeo* ("*works*") in Philippians 2:13? (p. 136)

   _____

7. What enables us to carry out God's good pleasure? (p. 136)

   _____

8. Complete this quote: "It takes _____ to love _____." (p. 137)

9. What is the meaning of the Greek word *katergazomai* ("*work out*") in Philippians 2:12? (p. 137)

   _____

10. By what are we defiled: what comes out of us or what goes into us? (p. 137)

_____

11. What is the meaning of *"treasure"* in Matthew 12:35? What idea is conveyed by "treasure" in the original Greek? (p. 137)

_____

_____

12. What is the gateway to our heart? (p. 138)

_____

13. In order to demonstrate the _____, _____, and _____
_____ of God, we must have already renewed our minds. (p. 138)

14. What is the meaning of the Greek word *anakainosis* (*"renewing"*) in Romans 12:2? (p. 138)

_____

15. What is the meaning of the Greek word *metamorphoo* in Romans 12:2? (p. 139)

_____

16. Describe how Jesus looked when He was transfigured. (p. 139)

_____

17. What is the meaning of the Greek word *metanoeo* (*"repent"*) in Acts 2:38? (p. 141)

_____

18. When sinners come to repentance, it means that they have changed their mind about _____,
about _____, and about their _____, recognizing their need for
_____. (p. 141)

19. To what does Jesus compare His ministry of calling sinners to repentance? (p. 142)

_____

20. Repentance is not merely about _____ _____ but about radical _____ _____. (p. 143)

21. When our _____ changes, our _____ will change. (p. 143)

22. What must we do in order to be able to fulfill the Great Commission? (p. 143)

_____

CONCLUSION

Mind renewal is the only way to truly experience the fullness of what God has promised us in His Word. It gives our new nature its full potency. This is how we work out our salvation as we walk in the Spirit. Our lives must be built and renovated according to the pattern of the living Word of God, the Lord Jesus Christ. When others see the splendor that is inside us, they will want God's manifest presence in their own lives.

APPLYING PRINCIPLES OF THE SUPERNATURAL

THINKING IT OVER

1. Consider these "Unlocking the Code of the Supernatural Insights" questions from page 144 of *Unlocking the Code of the Supernatural*:

   + What does it mean for us to "work out our salvation with fear and trembling"?

   + What is God's role in this process?

   + In Romans 12:2, what does the Greek word for *"renewing"* signify? How can we apply this concept to our lives?

   + What is the true meaning of repentance?

2. Have you built and renovated your life according to the pattern God provides? Are you living in a way that makes people want to ask who your Renovator is?

ACTING ON IT

1. What aspects of your life reflect a fleshly way of thinking? Make a list of them, then ask God to rebuild your life in ways that bring Him glory and manifest His power and blessings.

2. What is one thing you can do today to allow the light of the Holy Spirit within you to pierce the darkness?

PRAYING ABOUT IT

Father, in the name of Your Son Jesus Christ, I thank You that my inward life is Your priority. I praise You that You change me from the inside out. You are my holiness! I declare that Your Spirit is working within me to will and to do Your good pleasure. I work out my own salvation with fear and trembling. I decide to manifest what You have deposited within me. I repent from sin and from wrong ways of thinking. I declare that I think according to the Word of God, not according to religion and tradition. Father, use my life as a supernatural renovation project that draws people into Your kingdom and brings You glory. In Jesus's name, amen!

 AS WE RENEW OUR MINDS, WE WILL BE ABLE TO FULFILL THE GREAT COMMISSION, BRINGING MANY TO CHRIST AS WE DO MIRACLES, SIGNS, AND WONDERS IN HIS NAME!

CHRIST-CONSCIOUSNESS

CHAPTER THEME

The common misperception that the goal of being a Christian is to stop sinning causes many Christians to become angry, bitter, or discouraged. They may begin to see church as a sort of "spiritual car wash," where they can come to be washed clean, week after week, only to continue sinning. When we focus on our sinful state more than on our position of righteousness in Christ, we're practicing sin-consciousness. Instead, we must practice Christ-consciousness. The more we are conscious of Christ and His finished work on the cross, the more we will walk in victory in every area of our lives.

QUESTIONS FOR REFLECTION

1. Is your mindset usually one of sin-consciousness or Christ-consciousness? How can you become more Christ-conscious in your daily life?

2. Are you genuinely seeking to walk in victory? If not, what is holding you back?

3. How did you experience the Holy Spirit's conviction when you first came to know Christ?

4. When have you experienced godly sorrow?

EXPLORING PRINCIPLES AND PURPOSES

1. What do many people mistakenly think is the goal of a believer? (p. 145)

    _____

2. What is "sin-consciousness"? (p. 146)

    _____

    _____

3. God knows we need His _____ and _____ for our spiritual and emotional health. (p. 147)

4. What can result when pastors and spiritual leaders neglect to give believers godly affirmation according to the Word of God? (p. 147)

    _____

5. Define "The Law of Manifestation." (p. 147)

    _____

6. Complete this verse: *"For as he _____ in his heart, _____ _____ _____"* (Proverbs 23:7). (p. 147)

7. In 1 Corinthians 2, what was Paul determined not to teach the Corinthians? (p. 148)

    _____

8. What are two meanings for the Greek word *eido* (*"know"*) in 1 Corinthians 2:2? (p. 148)

    _____

9. Sin-consciousness focuses on _____, while Christ-consciousness focuses on _____. (p. 148)

10. What do most people mean when they say, "The Spirit convicted me"? (p. 149)

_____

11. There are three aspects to the Holy Spirit's assignment in the earth: He will *"reprove,"* or *"convict"* (NKJV), the world of (1) _____, (2) _____, and (3) _____. (p. 149)

12. What are some meanings for the Greek word *elegcho* (*"reprove"*) in John 16:8? (p. 149)

_____

_____

13. Jesus Christ sent the Spirit to convict _____ _____ of its sin. (p. 150)

14. When we were living according to the system of this world, who let us know that we were in unbelief? (p. 151)

_____

15. To whom does the second category of conviction that Jesus speaks about in John 16 apply? (p. 151)

_____

16. What is the meaning of the Greek word *dikaiosune* (*"righteousness"*) in John 16:10?

_____

17. Once we are born again, the Spirit convicts, or convinces, us of our _____ in Jesus. (p. 152)

18. In the third category of conviction, who does the Holy Spirit convince us has been judged by God? (p. 152)

_____

19. According to 2 Corinthians 7:10, what type of sorrow does the Holy Spirit produce within a believer? (p. 154)

_____

20. Godly contrition produces obedience. What does the sorrow of the world produce? (p. 154)

_____

21. By what is godly sorrow characterized? (p. 155)

_____

22. What is the meaning of the Greek term *apologia* ("*clearing*") in 2 Corinthians 7:11? (p. 155)

_____

CONCLUSION

Through Jesus's death, burial, and resurrection, the power of sin has been destroyed in the lives of born-again believers. Reproof, shame, guilt, and condemnation were never intended for those who are God's sons and daughters. The Holy Spirit convicts believers not of sin, but of our righteousness in Jesus, and He convinces us of our victory over the enemy. The Spirit stands with us and makes us conscious of the living Christ.

APPLYING PRINCIPLES OF THE SUPERNATURAL

THINKING IT OVER

1. Consider these "Unlocking the Code of the Supernatural Insights" questions from page 156 of *Unlocking the Code of the Supernatural*:

   + What is "The Law of Manifestation"? How can it bring either positive or negative results?

   + What are the three categories in which the Holy Spirit convicts?

   + Which of these categories apply to the world, and which apply to believers?

   + How does conviction in the life of an unsaved person differ from conviction in the life of a believer?

2. The Holy Spirit's conviction can be compared to a body of laws issued for people's safety and welfare. How does this analogy, found on page 152 of *Unlocking the Code of the Supernatural*, shape your thinking about what it means for the Holy Spirit to convict?

ACTING ON IT

1. Do you view God as a father who focuses on your mistakes instead of affirming you and communicating his love to you? If so, pray that God would correct this misperception and remind you of your identity as a cherished member of His family.

2. Consider some instances in your life when you have experienced what you identified as "conviction of sin." In those instances, were you genuinely repenting, or were you simply responding emotionally to your guilt and shame? Pray that God would give you discernment to distinguish between true conviction and emotions of guilt.

PRAYING ABOUT IT

Heavenly Father, I thank You for who You are and all that You have done for me. Help me to continually be Christ-conscious, rather than sin-conscious, so that I can walk in victory in every area of my life! Thank You that the Holy Spirit ministers to me to convince me of my righteousness in Jesus and to assure me that Satan has already been defeated. And thank You that, if I sin, Your grace produces godly sorrow within me so that I can immediately repent and experience inner transformation, having more and more love for You. In Jesus's name, amen!

 GODLY SORROW AND REMORSE DEMONSTRATE THAT WE DO NOT APPROVE OF OUR SIN. SUCH A DEMONSTRATION IS A GOOD SIGN THAT THE HOLY SPIRIT IS AT WORK IN OUR LIVES AND THAT WE ARE IN FACT BORN AGAIN.

THE MINISTRY OF THE HOLY SPIRIT

CHAPTER THEME

The Holy Spirit is not a force but a Person—the third person of the Trinity. Even though He is the most important Person in their lives, many believers know little about Him. The Holy Spirit is our Advocate who works not to condemn us for our sin but to comfort us in the truth of our righteousness in Christ. The Spirit points us to Jesus as our Redeemer and Source and guides us into all truth. Without the Holy Spirit, we cannot live lives of victory.

QUESTIONS FOR REFLECTION

1. How do you feel knowing that the Holy Spirit is your Advocate?

2. In what ways is the Holy Spirit teaching you and molding your character?

3. What does it mean that you are filled with the same Spirit that raised Jesus from the dead?

4. How would you describe the ministry of the Holy Spirit in your life?

EXPLORING PRINCIPLES AND PURPOSES

1. What does Genesis 1:2 describe the Holy Spirit doing at the beginning of creation? (p. 157)

   _____

2. Who anointed Jesus and gave Him the supernatural power to carry out His earthly ministry? (p. 157)

   _____

3. What was the Holy Spirit's role in Jesus's resurrection? (p. 157)

   _____

4. What is the Holy Spirit's role in salvation? (pp. 157–158)

   _____

   _____

5. The Holy Spirit possesses _____ _____, and He releases that _____ in our lives as we yield to Him. (p. 158)

6. Why is the Holy Spirit the most important Person in our lives? (p. 158)

   _____

7. In John 16:7, what does the Greek word *parakletos* ("*Comforter*") imply? (p. 158)

   _____

8. Real conviction reminds us of the holiness of God and produces _____ _____ in our hearts. Real conviction is rooted in _____-_____. (p. 158)

9.   Of what type of seed have believers been born again? (p. 159)

_____

10. What is one meaning of the Greek word *paideuo* ("*chastens*") in Hebrews 12:6? (p. 159)

_____

11. The Holy Spirit _____ us, _____ us, and _____ our character by reminding us and revealing to us what Jesus says. (p. 160)

12. For what reason has the Holy Spirit been given to the church? (p. 160)

_____

13. What is the meaning of the Greek word *phobos* ("*fear*"), and what English word derives from it? (p. 160)

_____

14. What does the Greek word *huiothesia* ("*adoption*") in Romans 8:15 indicate about our unique relationship with God? (p. 161)

_____

_____

15. The Holy Spirit operates within us and causes our spirits to cry, "_____ _____." (p. 161)

16. Why do believers always desire to please God? (p. 161)

_____

17. What is meant by the expression "joint witness"? (p. 161)

_____

18. What is the meaning of the Greek word *lupeo* ("*grieve*") in Ephesians 4:30? (p. 162)

_____

_____

19. The Holy Spirit will always remind us of our true identity, which is one of

"_____ *and* _____ _____" (Ephesians 4:24).

(p. 162)

CONCLUSION

Many believers live in a state of constant terror, afraid that God does not love them, and if they make one false move, He will strike them down. But these fears are not from God; they're from the enemy. Feelings of guilt and condemnation for sin also do not come from the Lord, and they do not bring Him glory. The Holy Spirit's mission is to lead us into truth and bring glory to Jesus. He is continually reaffirming the truth that we are heirs of God and joint-heirs with Christ.

APPLYING PRINCIPLES OF THE SUPERNATURAL

THINKING IT OVER

1. Consider these "Unlocking the Code of the Supernatural Insights" questions from page 163 of *Unlocking the Code of the Supernatural*:

   + What do believers have within them that prevents them from continuing in willful sin?

   + What is the Holy Spirit's mission in our lives?

   + What does it mean that we have received *"the Spirit of adoption"*?

   + In what way does the Holy Spirit "bear witness with our spirit"?

2. What does the knowledge that you are an adopted son or daughter of God mean to you?

ACTING ON IT

1. List the five attributes of the Holy Spirit discussed in this chapter. Then, circle the attribute that is most meaningful to you. Why did you circle that particular attribute?

2. Are you living in a state of constant fear in your faith walk? Write down your fears, then pray over each one, asking God to give you discernment to distinguish His loving truth from the enemy's lies.

Father, I thank You for who You are and all that You have done for me. Thank You for revealing to me the nature of Your precious Holy Spirit. Thank You, Holy Spirit, for leading me into all truth, which will transform my life. Thank You for being my Comforter and Guide. Lord Jesus Christ, I recognize that You are my Redeemer and Source. Through Your Spirit, I am convinced of my position of righteousness in You, and this revelation gives me the power to overcome sin in my life. Right now, I embrace the Spirit of Adoption. In Jesus's name, amen!

 AS NEW CREATIONS IN CHRIST, WE ARE FILLED WITH THE SAME SPIRIT THAT RAISED JESUS FROM THE DEAD. WE ARE SONS AND DAUGHTERS OF GOD WHO WALK IN RIGHTEOUSNESS AND ARE LED BY THE SPIRIT!

THE SPIRIT-FILLED LIFE

CHAPTER THEME

Many Christians have not yet embraced the foundational truth that God has called His church to be filled with the Spirit. Scripture demonstrates just how important the Holy Spirit is to believers. Indeed, being filled with the Spirit is not optional. God commands believers to be continually filled with the Holy Spirit.

QUESTIONS FOR REFLECTION

1. Are you being continually filled with the Spirit?

2. Why do so many believers today feel that they are less powerful than the believers in the early church were?

3. What does the Spirit-filled life look like?

4. How has your life changed since you received the baptism in the Holy Spirit?

EXPLORING PRINCIPLES AND PURPOSES

1. In what mood is the verb *pleroo* in Ephesians 5:18, and what does that signify? (p. 164)

   _____

2. Being filled with the Spirit is not _____. And it is not a _____-_____ event—it is a _____ filling. (p. 164)

3. In the book of Acts, what other type of filling do we see? (p. 165)

   _____

4. How do we know the outpouring of the Holy Spirit at Pentecost was important to Jesus? (p. 166)

   _____

5. What would the disciples have the power to do once they received the baptism in the Holy Spirit? (p. 166)

   _____

6. One meaning of the Greek word *dynamis* ("*power*") is "explosive power." What is another meaning? (p. 166)

   _____

   _____

7. What Greek word is translated as "*power*" in Luke 10:19, and what is another possible translation for this term? (p. 167)

   _____

8. _____ is an external endowment, whereas _____ is an internal capacity. (p. 167)

9. What is the meaning of the Greek term *baptizo* ("baptized") in Acts 1:5? (p. 168)

_____

10. When were Jesus's disciples submerged in the fire of the Holy Spirit? (p. 168)

_____

11. What ability were the disciples given when they were baptized in the Spirit? (p. 169)

_____

12. The gift of tongues enabled the early disciples to proclaim the message of God's kingdom with

_____, _____, and _____. (p. 169)

13. In what Old Testament book did God promise that He would pour out His Spirit on all flesh?
(p. 169)

_____

14. How many people were supernaturally convicted and added to the church following the outpouring on Pentecost? (p. 169)

_____

15. Speaking in tongues is not the main evidence or purpose of being filled with the Holy Spirit, although it is often the _____ evidence. (p. 169)

16. What is the role of speaking in tongues publicly? (p. 170)

_____

17. Who is the only Person who can unify the church? (p. 170)

_____

18. What are the meanings of the Greek term *martys* ("*witnesses*") in Acts 1:8, and what English word derives from this term? (p. 171)

CONCLUSION

The supernatural power of the Holy Spirit is to be demonstrated in every area of our lives. When we are filled with the same Spirit who raised Jesus from the dead, our lives are full of victory. When the third person of the Trinity is resident in our spirits, we have no reason to be defeated! We have heavenly power available to us at all times.

APPLYING PRINCIPLES OF THE SUPERNATURAL

THINKING IT OVER

1. Consider these "Unlocking the Code of the Supernatural Insights" questions from page 173 of *Unlocking the Code of the Supernatural*:

   • Is the command to be filled with the Holy Spirit optional? Why or why not?

   • List some meanings of the phrase "*be filled*" from the Greek word *pleroo* in Ephesians 5:18.

   • What are several purposes of the baptism in the Holy Spirit?

   • What "explosive combination" have we been given to release supernatural power in our lives?

2. In what ways would your life change if you were continually being filled with the Holy Spirit as commanded in Ephesians 5:18?

ACTING ON IT

1. Make a list of the effects of the baptism in the Holy Spirit that are discussed on pages 169–170 of *Unlocking the Code of the Supernatural*. Which effect is most meaningful to you? Why?

2. Pray that God would make every believer aware of the heavenly power that is available to us at all times through His Spirit.

PRAYING ABOUT IT

Father, I honor You today and praise You for who You are. I recognize that the Holy Spirit is the most important Person on earth because He reveals Jesus Christ to us and brings glory to the Father and the Son. Today, I desire to be filled with the Holy Spirit with the evidence of speaking in other tongues as the Spirit gives me utterance. I also receive the evidence and fruit of victorious living. From this day forward, I declare that I am a witness to the resurrection of Jesus Christ because of the Spirit's power at work in me. I operate in supernatural authority and power to transform the atmosphere around me. Through the Holy Spirit, I am enabled to walk in love, speak the truth, testify to You, and overcome sin in every area of my life. In Jesus's name, amen!

MIRACLE TESTIMONY

HEALED OF RHEUMATOID ARTHRITIS

We must always remember that everything the Father has given us is on the basis of Jesus's sacrifice on the cross and triumphant resurrection. This means that God has blessed us for Jesus's sake. God has forgiven us for Jesus's sake. God has healed us for Jesus's sake. We have a responsibility to recognize this spiritual reality and live according to it. Many people don't enjoy the abundant life because they insist on being justified or rewarded for their own righteousness and, sometimes, for their own "rightness."

This reminds me of the testimony of a woman whose body had been ravaged by rheumatoid arthritis. She was in excruciating pain all the time, unable to move her fingers or enjoy normal motor function. One day, in a healing meeting, I began to pray for such conditions. As this woman came to the altar, the Lord told me to lead people in a prayer of release and forgiveness. It turns out that this woman had been through a very nasty divorce and, as a result, had allowed bitterness and unforgiveness to creep into her heart. Because she had refused to forgive, she had been unable to receive her healing. However, the moment she released her husband and forgave him, she was instantly healed! Hallelujah!

Why did this happen? The woman finally let go of her "right" to be angry. And by letting go of her own righteousness, she was freed to receive what God had already provided for her.

The same principle applies to us. The moment we let go of our own righteousness, we can receive Christ's righteousness. This is a major key in unlocking the code of the supernatural.

 CAN YOU IMAGINE THE IMPACT THAT THE BODY OF CHRIST WILL HAVE ON THE WORLD WHEN WE ARE FILLED WITH THE LOVE AND POWER OF GOD?

ONE NEW MAN

CHAPTER THEME

In Ephesians 2:13, Paul says that we *"who sometimes were far off are made near by the blood of Christ."* God chose Abraham and made a covenant between him and his descendants for *"a thousand generations"* (see Psalm 105:8–10), commissioning Abraham to go and establish a new nation. This nation was composed of the Israelites, or the Jewish people. The Gentiles were a great distance away from God because they were outside of His original covenant with Israel. Yet when Christ shed His precious blood on the cross, He knocked down the barrier between Jews and Gentiles. No longer are Gentiles distanced from God. Through Christ, God created a new spiritual entity called the One New Man.

QUESTIONS FOR REFLECTION

1. In what ways can you thank God today that you have been brought near to Him in Christ, receiving full citizenship in His kingdom?

2. What does it mean to you that Jesus is our peace?

3. What is the significance of being part of the new spiritual entity called the One New Man?

4. Will you wake up and take your rightful place in the kingdom of God, walking in your true spiritual identity?

EXPLORING PRINCIPLES AND PURPOSES

1. To whom is Paul speaking in Ephesians 2:13, and to what is he referring? (p. 176)

   _____

2. To what concept do a number of Christians adhere, and what does this theological position assert? (p. 176)

   _____

   _____

3. God made a covenant between Abraham and his descendants for "_____ _____

   _____" (Psalm 105:8). (p. 176)

4. What is the meaning of the Greek term *makran* ("*far off*") in Ephesians 2:13 (NKJV), and what does it signify in Paul's discussion? (p. 176)

   _____

   _____

5. The Bible says that through Abraham (Israel), all the _____ of the earth would be

   _____. (p. 176)

6. What is the bridge that brought the Gentiles into covenant relationship with God? (p. 177)

   _____

7. What is the meaning of the Greek word *engys* ("*near*") in Ephesians 2:13, and to what can it refer? (p. 177)

   _____

8. Define the word *alien*. (p. 178)

    _____

    _____

9. Jesus Christ has become our Source of _____, _____, _____, _____, and _____ from rage and turmoil. (p. 178)

10. Under the new covenant, what has the blood of Jesus Christ become? (p. 178)

    _____

11. What illustrations did God use in His promise of blessing to Abraham? (pp. 178–179)

    _____

12. The word *"seed"* in Galatians 3 speaks of what two things? (p. 179)

    _____

13. Who comprises the *"one new man"* (Ephesians 2:15)? (p. 179)

    _____

14. To what does Paul refer when he speaks of *"enmity"* in Ephesians 2:15? (p. 180)

    _____

15. Those outside of God's covenant are the seed of the _____ _____. (p. 180)

16. What does it mean that we *"were by nature the children of wrath"* (Ephesians 2:3)? (p. 180)

    _____

17. The creation of One New Man means that, from a spiritual perspective, the _____ are _____. God no longer identifies us as _____. (p. 180)

18. Upon what foundation are we built? (pp. 181–182)

_____

19. What are the meanings of the Greek word *themelios* ("*foundation*") in Ephesians 2:20? (p. 182)

_____

20. Who is the Chief Cornerstone of the *"habitation of God"* (Ephesians 2:21), and who are the pillars? (p. 183)

_____

21. What is the revelation that was the *"rock"* (Matthew 16:18) upon which Jesus would build His church? (p. 184)

_____

CONCLUSION

Through Christ, God has literally created a new spiritual entity called the One New Man. Jew and Gentile have come together as a new creation. We are one in Christ! When we neglect this aspect of the new covenant, we miss out on the greatest revelation from God to His people since the world began. When we apply this revelation of our new nature, it will unlock more spiritual, physical, emotional, and financial blessings than the world has ever seen. If we want to see global awakening and revival come to the church, we must be fitly joined together.

APPLYING PRINCIPLES OF THE SUPERNATURAL

THINKING IT OVER

1. Consider these "Unlocking the Code of the Supernatural Insights" questions from page 185 of *Unlocking the Code of the Supernatural*:

    + What has the blood of Jesus Christ given Gentiles access to?

    + What does it mean that the *"middle wall of partition"* (Ephesians 2:14) that separated Jews and Gentiles has been removed?

- When we apply the revelation of the One New Man, what will unlock for us?

- How can we receive supernatural keys of authority?

2. What would it look like if the church were to see even greater results than were seen in the first-century church?

ACTING ON IT

1. Reread question 9 under "Exploring Principles and Purposes." What does Jesus give us by being "*our peace*" (Ephesians 2:14)? Which word in that list is most meaningful to you right now, and why?

2. Take some time to read Genesis 12–17 this week to learn more about the covenant God made with Abraham.

PRAYING ABOUT IT

Heavenly Father, thank You for the revelation of the One New Man! Thank You for creating a new spiritual entity by the miraculous union of Jewish and Gentile believers in Christ. May we all be "fitly framed together." As Your church applies this great revelation, may spiritual, physical, emotional, and financial blessings be unlocked for thousands of people. Let all nations of the world be blessed in Christ!

Thank You for bringing me, as one who was "far off," into Your covenant. Jesus, You are my Source of tranquility, security, safety, prosperity, and freedom from turmoil. I am stabilized empowered, secured, and blessed because of You. In Jesus's name, amen!

 THE GATES OF HELL WILL NOT PREVAIL AGAINST US! WHEN WE PRAY,
THE HEAVENS WILL OPEN! WHEN WE BIND THE ENEMY, HE WILL BE BOUND!
THIS IS THE POWER OF A UNITED CHURCH. THIS IS THE POWER OF THE ONE NEW MAN!

COMPLETE IN HIM

CHAPTER THEME

Many people in the body of Christ have been presented with an "incomplete gospel." Instead of being told how complete we are through the blood of Jesus, we are frequently told how incomplete we are. Often, the Christian leaders and other believers who present this message have good intentions. They want people to understand their need for Christ. However, they fail to move on to the fact of our newness and sufficiency in Him. Under Jesus's headship, rulership, and authority, we are complete. The moment we believe this truth, we will be catapulted into victory, power, and dominion.

QUESTIONS FOR REFLECTION

1. What role do you play in God's economy?

2. Have you been taught an "incomplete gospel"? If so, how has it affected your Christian walk?

3. What are the implications of being complete in Christ?

4. What does it mean to you that you can do greater works than Jesus did during His earthly ministry?

EXPLORING PRINCIPLES AND PURPOSES

1. Complete this quote of Colossians 2:10: *"And you are _____ in Him, which is the head of all principality and power."* (p. 186)

2. Who controls the factors of production in God's kingdom economy? (pp. 186–187)

    _____

3. What are the meanings of the Greek word *arche* (*"principality"*) in Colossians 2:10? (p. 187)

    _____

4. What do the Greek words *arche* and *exousia* imply when they are used together? (p. 187)

    _____

5. Jesus is _____ over any and all governments in the universe. (p. 187)

6. What are a few reasons why Christian leaders tell believers that they are incomplete? (p. 188)

    _____

    _____

7. God has already _____, _____, _____, and _____ us in Christ. (p. 188)

8. What is one result of the American church's tendency to promote convenience rather than encouraging us to work out our salvation? (p. 188)

    _____

9. Who is the key to worldwide revival? (p. 190)

    _____

10. What is the metaphorical meaning of the Greek word *kephale* ("head") in Colossians 2:10? What is the literal meaning? (p. 190)

_____

11. Christ is not a _____ to power. He _____ the power. (p. 190)

12. What is the Greek word translated *"more than conquerors"* in Romans 8:37, and what is one of its meanings? (p. 191)

_____

13. What is the meaning of the word *surpass*? (p. 191)

_____

14. We have experienced a "_____-_____" victory through Jesus. (p. 191)

15. How can we do greater works than Jesus did? (p. 191)

_____

16. How are we able to be "more than conquerors"? (p. 191)

_____

_____

17. In Romans 8:35, what does Paul say we are more than conquers of, and what do these things signify? (p. 191)

_____

_____

_____

18. You are not a _____ or a _____; you are a _____ and a _____!
(p. 192)

CONCLUSION

Christ is our Source of love, power, and validation. He is the One to whom we look for strength and security, and He is the One who makes us victorious. We are seated with God in heavenly places, and we have been given all authority in Christ. Always remember that you are complete in Jesus, and you are more than a conqueror through Him who loves you!

APPLYING PRINCIPLES OF THE SUPERNATURAL

THINKING IT OVER

1. Consider these "Unlocking the Code of the Supernatural Insights" questions from pages 193–194 of *Unlocking the Code of the Supernatural*:

    * List some meanings of *pleroo*, the Greek word translated *"complete"* in Colossians 2:10.

    * What are some characteristics and results of the "incomplete gospel"?

    * What does it mean to be "more than a conqueror"?

    * On what basis can we do greater works than Jesus did during His earthly ministry?

2. What does it mean that we carry Jesus's authority?

ACTING ON IT

1. While some Christian leaders preach that God is *about* to work in the lives of believers, in truth, God has already blessed, healed, forgiven, and prospered us in Christ. Circle the benefit from God listed in the previous sentence that is the most meaningful to you. Why did you circle that particular benefit? Take a moment to thank God for what He has already accomplished for you.

2. Are you ever frustrated by a lack of change in yourself or those around you? Pray that God would show you how to move out of His way and acknowledge Him as *the* power.

PRAYING ABOUT IT

Father, I praise and honor You because I am complete in Your Son Jesus Christ. Through Jesus, there is nothing missing and nothing broken in my life. I am whole. I acknowledge

Jesus as the Head over every principality and power, and over every name that is named. In Christ, I have been given the legal right to exercise dominion and authority in both the spiritual realm and the earthly realm. The devil is afraid of me because of who I am in You. Demons flee when I use the name of Jesus. I am so grateful that I am more than a conqueror through Christ Jesus who loves me. In Jesus's name, amen!

 YOU ARE MORE THAN A CONQUEROR THROUGH HIM WHO LOVES YOU!

ALL THINGS NEW

CHAPTER THEME

The mystery of our born-again nature comes down to one word: *new*. We are new creations! Yet many of us are uncomfortable thinking of ourselves in this way because we are fearful and uneasy about change. We are more comfortable with the familiar old nature, and we tend to be afraid of what we do not understand. But when we embrace our newness in Christ, we access God's supernatural power in remarkable ways.

QUESTIONS FOR REFLECTION

1. In what ways are you resisting seeing yourself as a new creation?

2. When have you found yourself trying to fight the evil nature you believed was still inside you?

3. What are some of God's great and precious promises through which you can partake of the divine nature?

4. What are some specific keys to unlocking the code of the supernatural you've learned in this book?

EXPLORING PRINCIPLES AND PURPOSES

1. What are some meanings for the Greek word *kainos* ("*new*") in 2 Corinthians 5:17? (p. 195)

    _____

2. What idea are "good angel, bad angel" cartoons trying to illustrate? (p. 196)

    _____

    _____

3. A born-again believer no longer posses what? (p. 196)

    _____

4. What is one of the most misunderstood theological truths in all of Christianity? (p. 196)

    _____

5. Complete this quote of 2 Corinthians 5:17: "*…all things are become* _____." (p. 197)

6. What is the meaning of the Greek word *physis* ("*nature*") in 2 Peter 1:4? (p. 197)

    _____

7. What does God share with us? (p. 197)

    _____

8. Partaking of God's nature is contingent upon what? (p. 197)

    _____

9. Complete this quote of Colossians 3:3: "*For you are* _____, *and your life is hidden with* _____ *in God.*" (p. 199)

10. In Romans 7:20, to what does Paul attribute the evil that arises in his life? (p. 200)

_____

11. We now live from a position of _____, not from a position of _____.
    (p. 200)

12. The Holy Spirit is a _____ _____ with the power to demolish sin
    in our lives! (p. 200)

13. You are not _____ but _____. You are not
    _____ but _____. You are not _____ but _____.
    (p. 201)

14. What words describe you because of the One who dwells inside you? (p. 201)

_____

15. What does the church need in order to overcome sin, sickness, poverty, and defeatism? (p. 202)

_____

CONCLUSION

Today is a new day. Today is the day that the Lord has made, and you can rejoice and be glad in it! The power of Jesus Christ resonates in your spirit. The same Spirit who raised Jesus from the dead lives in you, and He will give life to your mortal body. You are no longer a victim, no longer defeated, no longer broken. You have been restored to life, and God wants to use you for His glory. Get up! Start walking like the new person that God's Word says you are. From this day forward, there are no more limitations. Unlock the code of the supernatural in your life because today is a brand-new day!

THINKING IT OVER

1. Consider these "Unlocking the Code of the Supernatural Insights" questions from pages 203–204 of *Unlocking the Code of the Supernatural*:

   + What is "the-devil-made-me-do-it syndrome"? What is the truth regarding this mindset?

   + What are some meanings of the Greek word *koinonos*, which is translated as *"partakers"* in 2 Peter 1:4? Why is this word so significant for us?

   + List some of the attributes of God's nature that we have access to because His nature dwells within our spirit-man.

   + What is the supernatural mystery that was hidden for ages and is still being buried in the caverns of religion and tradition in our modern age?

2. Have you accepted what it means that the nature of God dwells within you?

ACTING ON IT

1. Think of a time when you've felt torn between your "good angel" and "bad angel." Pray that, the next time you struggle to obey God, the Lord will remind you that your old sinful nature has been abolished and help you to recognize that you have received a divine nature that gives you access to His unlimited victory and power in your life.

2. Review the list of God's attributes on page 199 of *Unlocking the Code of the Supernatural*. Which attribute is most meaningful to you? Why? Pray that God would show you in what ways you are partaking of this part of His nature.

PRAYING ABOUT IT

PRAYER OF SALVATION

Heavenly Father, I recognize that I am a sinner in desperate need of a Savior. I believe that Jesus Christ is Your Son. I believe that He suffered on the cross and died for me, descended into hell and defeated Satan, and now sits at Your right hand praying for me so that I may have abundant life. I am sorry for my sins; I repent of them and renounce them. Through the blood of Christ, I ask You to forgive me of all of my sins—those that are known to me and those that are unknown to me.

I receive Jesus as my Lord and Savior, and I give Him complete control over my life. I want to live for You from my innermost being and in every area of my life. I renounce Satan and all of his wicked works. I divorce myself from his evil influence. Lord, I recognize that I cannot live for You in my own strength. I ask You to fill me with Your precious Holy Spirit and give me the gift of speaking in other tongues, as the Spirit gives utterance, as the initial evidence of a transformed life. I ask this in the name of Your Son, Jesus Christ, amen!

 RISE, TAKE UP YOUR BED, AND WALK! FROM THIS DAY FORWARD, THERE ARE NO MORE LIMITATIONS. UNLOCK THE CODE OF THE SUPERNATURAL IN YOUR LIFE BECAUSE TODAY IS A BRAND-NEW DAY!

EXPLORING PRINCIPLES AND PURPOSES ANSWER KEY

CHAPTER 1

1. brand-new; supernatural
2. "something that is difficult or impossible to understand or explain"
3. "the secret counsels which govern God in dealing with the righteous, which are hidden from ungodly and wicked men but plain to the godly"
4. those who believe
5. the Holy Spirit
6. The church is not teaching or practicing the message of transformation.
7. new nature; living victoriously
8. understanding what it means to have a brand-new, supernatural nature
9. Christ comes to live within us in all His fullness.
10. Religion; tradition
11. He is the Word; He is God; He was with God in the beginning; He is the Creator; He is life; He is the light of men; He is the light shining in the darkness.
12. in the beginning; God; preexistent; coequal with the Father
13. "a word, uttered by a living voice, [that] embodies a conception or idea"
14. Jesus Christ
15. Form; purpose; substance
16. We must know who He is.
17. basic material; created; sustained
18. "to bring or band together"
19. source; bonding agent
20. "the absolute fullness of life, both essential and ethical, which belongs to God"
21. Creator; Definer; Purpose; Sustainer; Life; Light
22. that Jesus Christ shed His precious blood for our sins and was raised from the dead so that we could walk in supernatural newness of life in the power of the Holy Spirit

CHAPTER 2

1. something that has never before existed
2. "being in Christ"
3. in Christ; new creation
4. something that is "recently made, fresh...unused" and "of a new kind"
5. the spirit or spirit-man
6. the vital force by which our bodies are animated; our essential being, our true self
7. Father; Son; Holy Spirit
8. Our spirit-man unites with the Holy Spirit and becomes one with Him.
9. the Word of God
10. "the seat of the feelings, desires, affections, aversions (our heart, soul, etc.)"
11. the soul
12. affections; desires
13. take authority over our soul and body; our spirit can now direct our mind, will, and emotions, and our bodies can be conduits of righteousness
14. study God's Word to see what our new life looks like so the Holy Spirit can teach and guide us in the truth
15. study; meditate on
16. newness
17. without spot; blemish

CHAPTER 3

1. "a particular system of faith and worship"
2. "follower of Christ"; "imitator of Christ"
3. Antioch
4. "Jesus imitators"
5. identity; ritual
6. *"by the faith of the Son of God, who loved me, and gave Himself for me"*
7. Following Jesus is not the same as following a list of dos and don'ts.

8. in physical structures like the tabernacle and temple, within the ark of the covenant
9. in the spirit-man of the believer
10. the "Second Great Awakening"
11. evangelism and missions
12. what it means for us to have a relationship with God as His new creations
13. religious people; failed; broken; restored
14. the basis of what Christ has done for us
15. His very power is released in and through us.
16. They will be drawn to Him with awe and wonder.
17. Human beings desire to be glorified; they are prideful.
18. human doings; spiritual beings
19. We aren't following the sayings of a deceased religious leader; we are engaging with the very fullness of the Godhead embodied in the person of Jesus Christ.
20. religious; alive

CHAPTER 4

1. creating an atmosphere where nonbelievers would feel comfortable going to church and be able to relate to the message that were presented
2. looking the part; truly being born again
3. People do not know who they are.
4. a prominent religious leader (Pharisee); he acknowledged that Jesus had been sent by God
5. *born again*
6. *water; Spirit*
7. "to be begotten" or "to be fathered"
8. "and"
9. spiritual birth
10. We become children of God.
11. carnal; spiritual
12. the complex emotional and intellectual attributes that determine their characteristic actions and reactions
13. the *"power to become the sons of God"*
14. "to come into existence"; "become"; "made"
15. a disagreement between our spirit and our flesh
16. We want to obey God; we want to walk in His ways and fulfill His calling for us on this earth; we have an internal abhorrence of sin and anything that defies God.
17. *"I and My Father are one."*
18. one with Christ; one with the Father
19. guilt; shame; condemnation

20. from our secure identity in Christ
21. Jesus's living water
22. in spirit; in truth

CHAPTER 5

1. in reference to a system or worship
2. "clean"; "free from corrupt desire, from sin and guilt"; "free from every admixture of what is false; sincere; genuine"
3. spiritual disciplines; right motives
4. control over one's tongue
5. *the fatherless; widows*
6. "free from censure, irreproachable"
7. "devoid of force, truth, success, result" or "useless, of no purpose"
8. sinful, fleshy attitude; demonic influence
9. It promotes religious activity void of supernatural power and transformation; it causes people to say one thing and do another; it tries to mingle the things of God with the things of the world.
10. "piety toward God"
11. *dynamis*
12. believers; believers
13. 10 percent
14. the spirit of religion among the leaders and people in Jerusalem
15. mankind's shallow efforts to hide its sin and shame, to cover itself apart from God
16. barrenness
17. spiritual fruit
18. when we are intimate with Jesus Christ
19. "hypocrite"
20. deception
21. if we develop a habit of hearing the Word without doing the Word
22. "to forget"; "neglecting, no longer caring for"
23. barrenness; hypocrisy; deception

CHAPTER 6

1. a sect of Christians from the Jewish tradition that taught non-Jewish converts to Christ that they needed to be circumcised in order to be saved
2. the law; grace
3. a vicious cycle of bondage

4. "to traduce"; "to charm"

5. an emotionally abusive marital relationship

6. being pretentious; separating himself from Gentiles when he was near Jews; he was looking the part but not being the part

7. "to make great efforts to achieve or obtain something" or "to struggle or fight vigorously"

8. that Christ has already accomplished the work for us

9. grace; struggle

10. Holy Spirit

11. our fallen, carnal nature

12. when we consider them to be the means of our acceptance with God and if they are not directed by the Spirit

13. "to stand firm"; "to persevere"; "to keep one's standing"

14. finished work; spiritual reality

15. demonic forces

16. to fully accept God's unconditional love for us

17. We believe that we must perform flawlessly for Him to accept us.

18. volunteer at church; give to the poor; join church committees, boards, and ministries

19. perform; love

20. He sent His Son Jesus to die on the cross, be resurrected for us, and live victoriously within us through the Holy Spirit.

21. dead; dead

22. because we love Him through Jesus Christ

CHAPTER 7

1. the gospel of grace

2. for as long as he lived

3. to the law

4. the body of Christ

5. the moment we gave our lives to Jesus

6. sin; guilt; shame; condemnation

7. the very life and peace of God

8. "fruit to death" and "the oldness of the letter"

9. "the old state of life controlled by 'the letter'"

10. "a...bill, bond, account, written acknowledgement of a debt"

11. the moment Adam sinned against God

12. that they could not be righteous in themselves

13. magnifying glass

14. "the knowledge of things ethical and divine"

15. *Condemn* means "to declare to be reprehensible, wrong, or evil usually after weighing evidence and without reservation"; *katakrima* signifies a "damnatory sentence."

16. Unworthiness; love; mercy

17. our carrying a belief about ourselves that does not agree with the Word of God

18. no condemnation

19. They ran *from* God's presence rather than *to* His presence.

CHAPTER 8

1. *epignosis*; it is also found in Romans 3:20 in the phrase *"the knowledge of sin"*

2. of their true position in God, and of the way they ought to be

3. external works; spiritual positioning

4. We strive.

5. acceptance; favor; blessing

6. *the end of the law for righteousness*

7. the precious blood of the Lamb

8. your; Christ's

9. the gospel of Jesus Christ

10. righteousness of God

11. our faith in Christ

12. The sin of the entire world lay on His shoulders.

13. "to come into existence"; "to be finished"

14. the moment we gave ourselves to Jesus Christ

15. the eldest son; it was a decree of success, vision, and prosperity

16. Jacob received the blessing; Esau should have received the blessing because he was the firstborn.

17. He put on his brother's garments and wore goatskins on his arms and neck so they felt hairy like Esau's.

18. "to sink into (clothing), put on, clothe one's self"

19. Elder Brother

CHAPTER 9

1. Emperor Constantine

2. Protestantism, the Reformed Church, and the publication of the King James Version of the Bible

3. a Counter-Reformation

4. "the action or process of reforming an institution or practice"

5. It created an emphasis on *reformation* rather than *recreation*.

6. They focus on reforming people externally; churches should help believers understand what it means to be a new creation.

7. *renewed in knowledge*

8. Founder; "A New You"

9. the right to name the city, establish a government there, and build an infrastructure

10. spiritual transformation

11. They have not experienced authentic regeneration—or they are unaware of this spiritual change within them.

12. ambassadors; ministers

13. reformed; recreated

14. supernatural

15. *supernatural recreation*

16. as the salt of the earth and the light of the world

17. doorway; supernatural anointing

CHAPTER 10

1. thirty-eight years

2. We look for circumstances and external moves of God in which to place our confidence.

3. spirit; mind; body

4. *"Will you be made whole?"*

5. will

6. on his personal revelation of the unlimited power of Jesus Christ

7. *Rise; take up your bed; walk*

8. the spirit

9. "to arouse, cause to rise"; "to arouse from the sleep of death, to recall the dead to life"

10. spiritual death

11. life-giving power

12. death; life; carnal; spiritual

13. the soul

14. "raise up, elevate, lift up"; "to take upon one's self and carry what has been raised up"

15. sanctification

16. consecrating

17. *hagiasmos*; "holiness"

18. We need to change the way we think and reason to correspond with God's Word.

19. It is coming to the realization that we have already been raised together with Christ and made to sit together with Him in the heavenly places.

20. the natural life

21. past religious experiences

22. "to make one's way, progress; to make due use of opportunities"

CHAPTER 11

1. to manipulate them into trying to perform in order to earn God's love, acceptance, and validation

2. We live in a world where we are constantly reminded of people's pasts.

3. "original, primal, old, ancient"

4. the original or sinful nature we possessed apart from Christ

5. "to pass away, perish"

6. perished; abolished

7. *weak; wretched; poor; broken; lost; sinful*

8. *ambassadors for Christ*

9. all things new in Christ

10. couriers; mystery

11. If he can keep us focused on our sins, mistakes, and failures, he can successfully prevent us from walking as ambassadors of Christ.

12. God Himself, through His sacrifice of Christ

13. depths; sea

14. merciful; remember

15. to exonerate us of our sin and empower us to walk in righteousness

16. "given over to oblivion, i.e., uncared for"

17. that, because of their failings, they are no longer useful to God

18. past; future

19. "to run swiftly in order to catch a person or thing, to run after"; "to press on: figuratively of one who in a race runs swiftly to reach the goal"; "to pursue"

20. better promises

21. Jesus Christ

22. It was a time of remembering and accounting for all the sins the people had committed in the previous year.

23. God's compassion on His people

24. Christ the Messiah

25. because a knowledge of God and His ways has been placed inside of us

CHAPTER 12

1. good things; evil things
2. of eating without ceremonially washing their hands
3. dead
4. holy living as the ethos of the Christian message, which included refraining from certain behaviors and activities
5. It led them to essentially try to work out their salvation through outward actions and to overlook the essential gospel message.
6. "to be operative, be at work, put forth power"
7. God's power operating in us
8. God; God
9. "to perform, accomplish, achieve"; "to work out, i.e., to do that from which something results"
10. what comes out of us
11. our value system; it is what we hold near and dear; it refers to "the place in which good and precious things are collected and laid up"
12. our thought life
13. good; acceptable; perfect; will
14. "a renewal, renovation, complete change for the better"
15. "to change into another form, to transfer, to transfigure"
16. He took on another form; His face shined like the sun and His clothing became as white as light.
17. "to change one's mind"
18. God; themselves; sin; Christ
19. the process of putting wine into bottles
20. behavioral adjustments; inner transformation
21. thinking; lives
22. renew our minds

CHAPTER 13

1. to stop sinning
2. a frame of mind in which we invest most of our spiritual and mental energy on our sinful state, our failures, and our frailties rather than on our position of righteousness in Christ
3. love; affirmation
4. spiritual abuse
5. The things we continually set our mind on will ultimately manifest in our lives.
6. *thinks*; *so is he*
7. anything except Christ
8. "to discern"; "to pay attention"
9. us; Jesus

10. They feel bad about something they did wrong; their conscience is bothering them.
11. sin; righteousness; judgment
12. "to convict"; "to refute"; "to reprehend severely"; "to chide"; "to admonish"; "to call to account"
13. the world
14. the Holy Spirit
15. born-again believers
16. "the state of him who is as he ought to be"; "righteousness"; "the condition acceptable to God"
17. righteousness
18. *"the prince of this world,"* Satan
19. *"godly sorrow"*
20. death (separation from God)
21. a love for God and a hatred of sin
22. "a verbal defense"; "a speech in defense"

CHAPTER 14

1. "[moving] *upon the face of the waters*"
2. the Holy Spirit
3. He raised Jesus from the dead.
4. He is the regenerative Agent who quickens our dead human spirits, making us alive in Christ and joining us as one spirit with the Lord.
5. divine power; power
6. He is the One who reveals Jesus Christ to us and glorifies the Father.
7. that one of the Spirit's functions is that of Helper or "legal assistant"
8. reverential fear; Christ-consciousness
9. incorruptible seed
10. "to train children"
11. corrects; instructs; develops
12. to empower us to bring glory to God
13. "dread"; "terror"; *phobia*
14. We are His sons and daughters and have the full rights and privileges of one born into the family.
15. *Abba, Father*
16. because we are truly His children
17. Our spirits and the Holy Spirit both testify that we are God's children.
18. "to make sorrowful"; "to cause grief"; "to make one uneasy, cause him a scruple"
19. *righteousness; true holiness*

CHAPTER 15

1. It is in the imperative mood, so it is a command.
2. optional; one-time; continual
3. the baptism in the Holy Spirit
4. He instructed His disciples not to leave Jerusalem until they had received *"the promise of the Father."*
5. be witnesses for Jesus
6. "inherent power; power residing in a thing by virtue of its nature, or which a person or thing exerts and puts forth"
7. *exousia*; "authority"
8. Authority; power
9. "to immerse"; "to submerge"
10. on the day of Pentecost
11. the ability to speak in tongues
12. boldness; purity; conviction
13. Joel
14. three thousand
15. initial
16. It is a sign to unbelievers about the reality of God's presence and power.
17. the Holy Spirit
18. "one who is a spectator of anything, e.g., of a contest"; someone who can bear witness to the truth of something; *martyr*

CHAPTER 16

1. to Gentiles, referring to God's special covenant with Israel
2. Replacement Theology, which asserts that God's covenant with Israel no longer applies because Israel has been replaced by the church
3. *a thousand generations*
4. "far" or "a great way"; it signifies that the Gentiles were a great distance away from God because they were outside of His original covenant with Israel
5. nations; blessed
6. the blood of Christ, the Messiah
7. "near, of place and position"; can refer to "those who have near access to God"
8. a foreigner who does not have political, social, or economic rights and benefits in the country in which they live
9. tranquility; security; safety; prosperity; freedom

10. the eternal peace treaty between Jews and Gentiles
11. stars and sand
12. Abraham's physical descendants and Jesus Christ
13. Jews and Gentiles
14. the spiritual hostility that Gentiles had toward God and His people
15. wicked one
16. We were prone to reject God and violate His ordinances.
17. two; one; separate
18. the apostles and prophets
19. "the foundations, beginnings, first principles" of "an institution or a system of truth"
20. Jesus Christ; apostles and prophets
21. that Jesus was *"the Christ, the Son of the Living God"*

CHAPTER 17

1. complete
2. the King Himself, Jesus
3. "principality"; "rule"; "magistracy"
4. a kingdom or government
5. Head
6. They want people to understand their need for Christ, they don't believe they themselves are complete in Christ, or they want to fuel their own "religious system."
7. blessed; healed; forgiven; prospered
8. Many Christians are "conveniently" bound, addicted, perverted, and disobedient to God.
9. Jesus Christ
10. "anything supreme, chief, prominent"; the physical head
11. means; is
12. *hypernikao*; "to gain a surpassing victory"
13. "to exceed"; "to be greater than"
14. greater-than
15. because we have the indwelling Christ inside of us
16. We are in a relationship with Jesus; we carry Jesus's authority and operate in His power.
17. tribulation; distress; persecution; famine; nakedness; peril; sword; they are the circumstances and spiritual forces that seek to separate us from the love of Christ, and they are the situations of our lives that attempt to throw us into an identity crisis
18. pauper; beggar; king; priest

CHAPTER 18

1. something that is "recently made, fresh… unused"; "of a new kind"
2. the idea that mankind has a good nature and a bad nature, and our choices are determined by one or the other
3. a sinful nature
4. that, although our body and our flesh have remained the same, our spirit-man has become new and always desires to please God
5. new
6. "the sum of innate properties and powers by which one person differs from others"
7. His own nature—His "innate properties and powers"
8. our recognizing and applying His promises
9. *dead; Christ*
10. to sin that dwells inside his flesh
11. power; weakness
12. spiritual bulldozer
13. incomplete; complete; unrighteous; righteous; old; new
14. holy; righteous; redeemed; saved; sanctified; empowered; faithful; blessed
15. "Christ in us"

ABOUT THE AUTHOR

Dr. Kynan T. Bridges is the senior pastor of Grace & Peace Global Fellowship in Tampa, Florida. With a profound revelation of the Word of God and a dynamic teaching ministry, Dr. Bridges has revolutionized the lives of many in the body of Christ. Through his practical approach to applying the deep truths of the Word of God, he reveals the authority and identity of the new covenant believer.

God has placed on Dr. Bridges a particular anointing for understanding and teaching the Scriptures, along with the gifts of prophecy and healing. Dr. Bridges and his wife, Gloria, through an apostolic anointing, are committed to equipping the body of Christ to live in the supernatural every day and to fulfill the Great Commission. It is the desire of Dr. Bridges to see the nations transformed by the unconditional love of God.

A highly sought speaker and published author of a number of books, his previous books with Whitaker House include *School of the Miraculous*, *Invading the Heavens*, *Unmasking the Accuser*, *The Power of Prophetic Prayer*, and *Kingdom Authority*. Dr. Bridges is a committed husband, a mentor, and a father of five beautiful children: Ella, Naomi, Isaac, Israel, and Anna.